SURGING DEMOCRACY

SURGING DEMOCRACY

Notes on Hannah Arendt's Political Thought

ADRIANA CAVARERO

Translated by Matthew Gervase

STANFORD UNIVERSITY PRESS
Stanford, California

STANFORD UNIVERSITY PRESS
Stanford, California

English translation ©2021 by the Board of Trustees of the Leland Stanford Junior University. All rights reserved.

Surging Democracy: Notes on Hannah Arendt's Political Thought was originally published in Italian in 2019 under the title *Democrazia sorgiva: Note sul pensiero politico di Hannah Arendt* ©2019, Raffaello Cortina Editore.

Preface ©2021 by the Board of Trustees of the Leland Stanford Junior University. All rights reserved.

No part of this book may be reproduced or transmitted in any form or by any means, electronic or mechanical, including photocopying and recording, or in any information storage or retrieval system without the prior written permission of Stanford University Press.

Printed in the United States of America on acid-free, archival-quality paper

Library of Congress Cataloging-in-Publication Data
Names: Cavarero, Adriana, author. | Gervase, Matthew, translator.
Title: Surging democracy : notes on Hannah Arendt's political thought / Adriana Cavarero ; translated by Matthew Gervase.
Other titles: Democrazia sorgiva. English
Description: Stanford, California : Stanford University Press, 2021. | Translation of the author's Democrazia sorgiva. | Includes bibliographical references and index. |
Identifiers: LCCN 2020052615 (print) | LCCN 2020052616 (ebook) | ISBN 9781503627499 (cloth) | ISBN 9781503628137 (paperback) | ISBN 9781503628144 (ebook)
Subjects: LCSH: Arendt, Hannah, 1906-1975. | Democracy. | Political science—Philosophy.
Classification: LCC JC251.A74 C3813 2021 (print) | LCC JC251.A74 (ebook) | DDC 321.8--dc23
LC record available at https://lccn.loc.gov/2020052615
LC ebook record available at https://lccn.loc.gov/2020052616

Cover design: Rob Ehle

Cover photo: Collage out of one photo of Black Lives Matter protest, June 2, 2020, New York City. Original photo from Evan Agostini/Invision/AP.

Text design: Kevin Barrett Kane

Typeset at Stanford University Press in 10/14 Minion Pro

... these are exercises in political thought
as it arises out of the actuality of political incidents ...
Hannah Arendt, *Between Past and Future*

Contents

	Preface to the English Edition	ix
	QUARTET **Surging Democracy**	1
1	The Idea of Democracy	3
2	Plurality	15
3	Public Happiness	30
4	Political Squares	45
	DUO **Political Phonospheres**	57
5	The Voice of the Masses	59
6	The Voice of Plurality	72
	SCHERZO **Crowds with a Cellphone**	87
7	Crowds with a Cellphone	89
	Notes	97
	Index	109

Preface to the English Edition

History is always unpredictable, as Hannah Arendt has said, but sometimes its rapid pace takes us particularly by surprise. Here, I will give a personal narrative of it by focusing on the period between the publication of the Italian edition of this book and the present moment of writing this preface. Less than ten months.

Democrazia sorgiva had just been published in Italy, in October 2019, when, a few weeks later, the new "Sardines" movement was suddenly packing Italian piazzas with thousands of people protesting the antimigrant, sovereigntist, and hate-speech propaganda of the Lega, a right-wing party competing in the impending regional elections, whose political leader, Matteo Salvini, was dominating the populist vote in Italy's polls.

The Sardines phenomenon was a notable one, quickly proliferating in cities and towns, from north to south, and inundating the media and the news. Observers were puzzled by the totally nonviolent behavior of such a large number of people, of every age and social condition, joyously gathering in public spaces to fill them up with their bodies, like sardines. Although the Sardines explicitly opposed the spreading of racism, intolerance, and hatred among the supporters of a populist leader fomenting hostility toward ethnic minorities and fueling prejudices and resentments, the piazzas crowded with Sardines were not framed by the typical marks of protest and struggle, and even less by rage and insurgency, but rather by the thrilling emotion of participating in political demonstrations within a shared public space.

I must confess that, by joining the Sardines and singing the mid-twentieth-century antifascist anthem "Bella Ciao" together with thousands of people assembled in the piazza, I too felt this emotion. And, on a strictly personal level, I was excited by the perception that the Sardines were rediscovering and experiencing that form of plural, horizontal, nonviolent, generative, and affirmative interaction, which, revisiting the Arendtian notion of politics in this book, I call "surging democracy."[1] Needless to say, my emphasis here falls on a local phenomenon, on events that occurred in Italy and were a source of personal intellectual satisfaction.

The concept of surging democracy that I discuss in this book, however, goes far beyond this particular setting, engaging with a variety of historical phenomena that regularly occur wherever people, by gathering in public spaces to protest or demonstrate, experience their ability to engender power—a diffuse, participatory, and relational power, shared equally, or better still, a power constituted by political actors who are unique and plural. It is the one situation, Arendt points out, in which we can experience "public happiness." As such, she suggests, it pertains to certain happy phases of revolutions, notably the American Revolution, when the movement of insurgency and protest, often violent and aimed at *liberation*, is suspended, allowing the human taste for *freedom* and emotional participation to surface. In truth, the boundaries between the struggle for liberation and the direct experience of freedom are often blurred, as Arendt notes. Moreover, she warns that it is frequently very difficult to say where the mere desire for liberation, to be free from oppression, ends, and the desire for freedom as the political way of life begins. Yet, when people gathering in protest and fighting for liberation happen to savor the taste of a democracy-in-the-making in its nascent stage, they do recognize it as a distinct and thrilling experience of political freedom.

Commenting on the Italian squares packed with Sardines, columnists and critics at the time accused the movement of being naïve and superficial, lacking an effective political agenda. What do the Sardines want, they argued, besides an understandable protest against a populist demagogue who has large popular support, and against the devastating effects of his vicious rhetoric? Which party or institutional project do the Sardines support, beyond appealing to general issues like those of equality and inclusion, respect for differences, and responsible public language?

However, this line of thinking missed the political core of the phenomenon, that is, its being a manifestation of a specific, performative type of politics that is enacted when people congregate, reclaiming a public space, or, to borrow Judith Butler's terminology, when, in order to protest, bodies gather in a shared space, displaying the protestors' corporeal plurality. Tellingly, the political performance of the Sardines lay in their very name, that is, in the physical relationality of bodies that fill public squares and enjoy the political experience of this interactive fulfillment. By gathering, they disclosed the significance of their main claims, which affirmed: We are plural, each an embodied uniqueness, distinct and equal, rejecting exclusion and enacting inclusion. We embrace and empower differences. We display differences in flesh and blood, freed of the political and cultural game of rejection. We congregate bodily to protest segregation and racism. And there is happiness in experiencing and sharing the public exhibition of our incarnate plurality. There is joy in physically engendering freedom.

Then came the coronavirus and, all of a sudden, the squares were empty. Nobody, no-body there. Everybody in lockdown. Then came the social distancing, which in fact is a physical distancing: distancing of bodies. Neither joy nor happiness, but fear, mourning, and grieving. Notwithstanding the initial shock, Italians responded to the required mandate of physical distancing by singing together from balconies and windows, their voices joining and sounding in the emptied squares and streets. They sang popular songs, above all "Bella Ciao," a chant of resistance and hope, linked to the liberation from fascism. Commenting on this vocal phenomenon, Bonnie Honing has insightfully spoken of a "serenade for democracy." We did miss democracy, but not the democratic government ruling the country, which was working well enough and doing its best to face the contagion, also because Italy provides universal health care access to all. We missed the recent experience of surging democracy, the thrill of congregating in public spaces, the square packed with thousands of bodies, the taste for freedom in the form of physical relationality. Once again bodies were at center stage, now not because of their urge to congregate and actively perform the political significance of plurality, but because of their being the very vehicle of contagion, the spreading of which feeds on assembled bodies, their physical relation, contact, their breath and touch, in proximity.

In light of the rapid time sequence that replaced the experience of surging democracy with the necessity of physical distancing, the situation in Italy indeed seemed paradoxical. Now bodies, prohibited from political interaction in a shared public space, started to perform, isolated in private rooms, a public ethics of care: care for the health of others, given that every singular body could be contagious and infect other bodies. As epidemiologists and scientists made clear, physical distancing and wearing masks, rather than serving the individual instinct of self-preservation, in fact protect the community from contagion, first and foremost the fragile bodies of the elderly and of those who are particularly vulnerable because of their health or social condition. Caring about the most vulnerable bodies during the pandemic has meant physically distancing oneself while ethically empowering the corporeal dimension of human relationality.

There were, of course, people who embraced this ethical commitment actively, engaging in volunteer action and mutual aid. Moreover, there were caregivers of a special kind, practicing public ethics in its most essential form: doctors, nurses, paramedics, and other health care workers, whom people in lockdown celebrated with choruses of applause and songs from windows and balconies. "Our angels," they were called. Columnists and critics did not miss the opportunity of accusing Italians of romanticizing "heroes" and extolling their "courage." Yet the applause was far from a simple regression to traditional folklore attitudes. It was difficult to reconcile a certain emphasis on our ethical "sacrifice" of staying at home, in order to care for the bodies of others, and the impressive performance of exhausted workers, at the brink of personal collapse and at risk to their own lives, taking care of infected bodies in hospitals and intensive care wards. We perceived that their public ethics of care, their inclination toward others, their bending over vulnerable human bodies, was quite intensive, and we applauded and sang out of solidarity and gratitude.

Then the number of victims and the pandemic spreading worldwide rendered us mute. Awareness arose, everywhere, of the event's unprecedented historical dimension and of the changes affecting our "normal" lives, perhaps also an opportunity for rethinking human life, its vulnerability and livability, along with the political community and the natural environment we are part of. As a matter of fact, the environment benefited immensely from the lockdown, while the human world seemed to freeze and disappear. Venice's canals had crystal-clear water in which octopuses danced for the first time in hundreds of years. No people were on the street in New York, while Central Park was blooming more gorgeously than ever. Some of us were amazed at the beauty of these surreal scenarios, feeling guilty for enjoying the view of a world without humans. Many, however, had to cope with the nostalgia of the human world as we knew it.

Then the more usual human world resurfaced, presenting us with its all too familiar ugly face, that of racial murder. On May 25, in Minneapolis, George Floyd, an African-American man, was killed by a police officer who pressed a knee on the back of his neck for eight minutes and forty-six seconds. A video of the killing circulated worldwide, in which Floyd could be heard repeatedly saying, "I can't breathe." Suddenly "I can't breathe" became the rallying cry of thousands of people taking to the streets and filling public squares, in the United States and across the globe, protesting structural racism and police brutality, the old sin of America, the persisting sin of democratic American history. "Cumulative rage, despair, and grief surged like a tidal wave," read the *New York Times*, resulting in "one of the most explosive trials of American racism in modern times." Despite the worldwide lockdown, which kept billions of people at home, in the United States and elsewhere bodies started to inundate public spaces again. A sudden and spreading rage against injustice, inequality, and the daily hardships faced by African-Americans was at the core of the new demonstrations, along with the unresolved legacy of slavery haunting American democracy from its foundation.

It was perhaps the first time in history that thousands of bodies gathering in protest confronted the reality of a pandemic that called for physical distancing. Nevertheless, they marched together, sang and shouted with urgent voices muffled behind masks. In most cities the demonstrations were peaceful. In several cases, the protesters wore masks and tried to enact an unprecedented political performance by situating thousands of bodies at a distance within the public space they shared. In other cases, people took a knee and whispered for eight minutes and forty-six seconds, "I can't breathe." This happened in Italy, too, including during a demonstration held in an old piazza in Verona, in which I participated. In Berlin an estimated fifteen thousand protesters filled Alexanderplatz with signs that read, "Germany is not innocent." In Bristol the statue of a slave trader, Edward Colston, was ripped from its plinth and thrown into the harbor, while in Belgium protesters targeted memorials to Leopold II, the Belgian king who made Congo his own genocidal private property. Many other removals of statues occurred across Europe and the United States.

Columnists and critics, along with some political leaders, argued that tearing down statues means lying about history. Yet history does not consist of more-or-less neutral chronicles of facts and events, but, as Walter Benjamin taught us, it is instead made up of the victors' hegemonic narratives about these facts and events. Instruments of simplification and celebration, statues illustrate the historical tale of the winners. By standing erect in public spaces of appearance, they consolidate and transmit the winners' account of the progress of history, no matter if such a progress entailed deportation, enslavement, or extermination of entire populations. Statues in public places are conspicuous, if not provocative.

Maybe the tearing down of statues is not a central point within the international phenomenon of the Black Lives Matter movement protesting police violence and structural racism in the United States and other western democratic countries. It works, however, as a symbolic gesture inviting current democracies to eventually come to terms with their hegemonic narrations of history—sometimes, literally, a monumental history. The past cannot be undone, but its narration and monumental illustration can. Actually, the sign reading "Germany is not innocent" was immediately understood by the people in Berlin. While regularly interrogating its Nazi past—and at the same time facing the recent resurgence of a neo-Nazi party—Germany does not fail to do the same with its colonial past. An exhibition held in 2017 at the German Historical Museum in Berlin detailed and documented in-depth German genocidal racism in Africa. On the other hand, while demonstrating in Italian piazzas for Black Lives Matter, we knew in a special way what "I can't breathe" meant, given that by pronouncing that sentence we cannot help thinking of the thousands of migrants who, leaving the African shores on rubber boats doomed to sink, suffocate daily in the waters of the by-now marine cemetery of the Mediterranean sea, while the European coastal states go on arguing about which of them is supposed to send rescue ships or welcome them in its ports. When Salvini ruled in Italy as interior minister a few years ago—Salvini, the same populist leader the Sardines were contesting in their joyful squares—he closed Italy's ports to ships carrying rescued migrants. Truly, the issue of migrants' lives and other lives that matter less or do not matter—lives that are not grievable as Judith Butler would say—is a particularly urgent one, entrenched in the very core of democracy, whatever we intend by this name.

It is difficult to speak of the present and interpret it philosophically. While I am writing this preface, some scholars are speaking of the pandemic as a catastrophic event, affecting history on a global level, which will change our lives and impact the consolidated, geopolitical patterns of society and the economy. With regard to the international diffusion of the movement protesting structural racism in the United States and elsewhere, other scholars speak of a political event that calls America and Europe, along with democracy itself, into question. One could also simply say that, in times of change, the time has come for current democracies to rediscover the ideas and practices that originated them at the threshold of modernity. Tellingly, when she speaks of America, Arendt links this origin to the experience of revolution, intending it as the communal experience of political freedom that eventually should become "constituted" in new political institutions.

No matter how these constituting attempts have failed historically, we must keep in mind that history is unpredictable, indeed, it never stops occurring and surprising us. Things keep happening. Maybe we happen to live in a time when liberal democracies are historically compelled to confront both the racial pathology that structurally affects them and the experience of surging democracy from which they stemmed and by which they were constituted. If it is true, as Arendt claims, that attempts at constituting freedom cannot exist without interaction in public horizontal spaces, shared by citizens who actively display that ontological condition of plurality that makes them unique and equal, perhaps we can look at the actual demonstrations for Black

Lives Matter through a certain lens of political hope. Systemic racism, beyond being a human shame, is structurally incompatible with the very concept of democracy. The revolutionary experience from which modern democracies arose consists of a plural, horizontal interaction that makes inclusion its material kernel and exclusion a logical contradiction. Inasmuch as the thousands of people protesting racism and crowding the squares with the rallying cry "I can't breathe," in a time of pandemic, exhibited their embodied plurality in public spaces of appearance in order to claim justice and equality, they exhibited the original human taste for freedom, too, and, along with this taste, notwithstanding their rage and indignation, they experienced the familiar thrill of interacting with each other. It is a democratic thrill, consistent with the collective emotion of participating in the nascent stage of democracy, that germinal form of diffuse, equally shared and inclusive power, which alone, according to Arendt, deserves the name of politics.

I know that my present analysis, tentative and provisional as it can be in times of historical accelerations, risks running off toward utopia while calling on an imaginary of hope. But there is no historical change without hope, and perhaps there is no action either. In order to change, to let things happen for the better, to overcome racism and inequality, to rediscover the birthing core of democracy and turn the shared experience of freedom into constituted social and political institutions, we do need an imaginary of hope. After all, as Arendt says, political changes enacted by the rediscovery of freedom, although unpredictable, keep resurfacing in history with "an utmost weird precision."

Verona, August 2020

SURGING DEMOCRACY

QUARTET

Surging Democracy

1 The Idea of Democracy

THE ANCIENT GREEKS, when speaking of democracy, "conceived of it as a public square or an assembly in which citizens were called upon to make decisions that directly concerned them,"[1] writes Norberto Bobbio. In its simplicity, this image continues to inspire our fundamental understanding of democracy. To aid our discussion, we might appeal to the term *direct democracy*. But then we would risk making democracy no longer an idea—a schema, a mental perspective, a conceptual framework—but rather a precise form of government; or rather, to use our modern political lexicon, a certain type of political regime distinct from "representative democracy." The idea of democracy, which we will explore in this work, does not fit any of these classifications. It is not limited to a model of government defined by principles, rules, or procedures, nor to a system of values. It belongs, rather, to the phenomenology of political experience; more precisely, if we persist with the image of the polis, to the specific political experience of antiquity which was based upon the physical sharing of a common space—the famous *agorà*—in which free individuals interacted as equals. In this sense, democracy is more than a form of government originating in Greece and then reappearing in a number of historical variations until it was incorporated into the modern forms of representative democracy. Prior to any form of government, the word democracy evokes a certain spatial arrangement, a horizontal plane for the interaction of equals. To describe it in the vocabulary of Hannah Arendt, it evokes a communal space of reciprocal appearance, where a plurality of unique beings acts in concert.

Arendt is not mentioned here by chance. Her texts not only still retain today the extraordinary quality of offering relevant commentary for anyone engaged with urgent political problems, so much so that one often has "a strange sense that Arendt's work speaks directly to events of ours";[2] but, even more importantly, references to Arendt's texts are frequent among numerous political theorists of our own time who are again interrogating the very idea of democracy in order to tease out its meaning in present events. We are referring specifically to those theorists looking to reclaim the word democracy from annoying generalizations, and who are attempting to grasp the conceptual core of "true democracy."[3] This applies, first of all, to the version of "radical democracy" proposed by Judith Butler, but also to the notion of "anarchic democracy" that Jacques Rancière explores, or even to the concept of "insurgent democracy" elaborated by Miguel Abensour,[4] whose work also touches upon Claude Lefort's idea of "wild [*sauvage*] democracy." Actually, given that he engages with Arendt in a particularly fruitful way, Lefort can be considered as the principal author who opened up this varied stream of theoretical inquiry characterized by a commitment to radicalizing the idea of democracy by conceiving of it in terms of permanent conflict and as a field of struggle.[5] In France above all, this current is not only varied but also well established, able to account for, among other things, Étienne Balibar's project of the "democratization of democracy," as well as the agonistic concept of democracy proposed by Chantal Mouffe.[6] Without entering here into the details of the complex and diversely articulated thought of these authors, it is worth pointing out their need to add an adjective to the noun democracy, qualifying it as radical, anarchic, insurgent, wild, agonistic. Abensour writes, "if left undelineated, democracy would risk losing any identifiable features, and would be swept away into the greyness of universal trivialization; is it not constantly confused in the everyday language of contemporary society with the rule of law or representative government?"[7]

In a more general sense, the necessity of including an adjective indicates the difficulty of speaking of democracy, now as in the past, without running the risk of the word immediately designating a form of government, a political regime, a certain institutional structure, if not a type of lifestyle or social organization. Even ordinary political language tends to adjectivize democracy, defining it, depending on circumstances, as representative, liberal, parliamentary, popular, electoral, formal, real, or any other number of forms. Arendt, by contrast, rarely uses the term democracy. While praising democratic Periclean Athens as the birthplace of that experience of plural interaction that she identifies with the authentic and original notion of politics, she avoids any recourse either to the word democracy or, even more so, to the expression direct democracy. She does, on rare occasions, in minor texts and with a clear intent to simplify, use the expression "participatory democracy," placing it in quotes.[8] Indeed, what we have here called the "idea of democracy" corresponds directly, in Arendt's terminology, to the idea of politics or, better yet, to "a pure concept of what constitutes the political."[9] It is not simply a lexical issue, even if lexical issues, obviously, are important. It is also a question of understanding why so many of the authors who today are trying to radicalize the idea of democracy refer to Arendt, who avoids even using the term.

An extended quotation from Arendt's *On Revolution* can shed some light on this paradox:

> Freedom as a political phenomenon was coeval with the rise of the Greek city-states. Since Herodotus, it was understood as a form of political organization in which the citizens lived together under condition of no-rule, without a division between rulers and ruled. This notion of no-rule was expressed by the word isonomy, whose outstanding characteristic among the forms of government, as the ancients had enumerated them, was that the notion of rule (the "archy" from *archein* in monarchy and oligarchy, or the "cracy" from *kratein* in democracy) was entirely absent from it. The polis was supposed to be an isonomy, not a democracy. The word "democracy", expressing even then majority rule, the rule of the many, was originally coined by those who were opposed to isonomy and who meant to say: What you say is "no-rule" is in fact only another kind of ruler-ship; it is the worst form of government, rule by the demos.[10]

It is important to note here the repeated emphasis on the absence of rule. It is precisely this absence of division between the rulers and the ruled that characterizes what the Greeks called *isonomia* and which, throughout her work, Arendt instead calls politics, by which she means the shared space of interaction between equals. The term rule or government has, for her, a negative connotation, so much so that she often uses it as a synonym for "domination" (*Herrshaft*), that is, a system in which some rule and others are ruled. Arendt is clear in her description of the "realm of power struggles in which nothing is so much at stake as the question of who rules over whom,"[11] that realm which the western tradition, from Plato onward, instead calls, and according to Arendt, incorrectly, politics. The word politics, as it is employed in the western tradition in reference to problems of power and rulership, is by Arendt considered misleading and false insofar as it conceals and supplants the original experience of the polis, thus stifling the genuine political spirit of the Greek citizen who wanted "neither to rule nor to be ruled."[12] According to Arendt's vision, there is no politics where what is at stake is who rules and who is ruled, who governs and who is governed: and this explains why, when speaking of the true meaning of politics, she avoids using the word democracy. But it also explains why her specific understanding of politics could not but be of interest to all those who are currently striving to valorize the idea of democracy, adjectivizing it as radical, anarchic, insurgent, wild, or agonistic. What these authors appreciate, within the Arendtian perspective, is indeed the exaltation of a certain type of political experience, which positions itself as antithetical to any vertical or hierarchical conception of power, and that is instead characterized as a diffuse, participatory, and relational power, shared equally, or better still, constituted by a plurality of actors. These are equals precisely because they share a common space in a horizontal sense.

It is not by chance, for that matter, that Arendt's idea of politics insists primarily upon a spatial dimension, without placing any particular emphasis on the theme of self-determination, which stands out in the definition of Bobbio, quoted above. Politics, writes Arendt, entails a plurality of actors who are simultaneously equal and distinct, and arises "*between* men to the extent that they move within the ambit that lies *between* them."[13] It is precisely this in-between that constitutes a physical space of participation, which

1: The Idea of Democracy

the Greeks "discovered." Its aim consists in enacting a relationship between those who are present, allowing them to mutually appear and remain distinct, unique human beings who do not melt into a uniform mass. Arendt adds that the Greek discovery of "the essence and the realm of the political" did not just concern an experience tied to the physical space of the *agorà*,[14] but was expressed and actualized in an entirely unique way of life, the *bios politikos*, a particular way of being that realized to its fullest potential the human condition of plurality. For Arendt, in originally Greek political experience, and consequently in politics correctly understood, what is at stake is precisely the human, that is, a specific mode of interacting in a public space, where people "appear to each other" as unique and beginners, "from which no human being can refrain and still be human."[15] The tone, at times been noted by critics, comes across as overemphatic. One must not, however, lose sight of the dramatic historical context in which Arendt's writing took shape: it is in response to the totalitarian catastrophe, which she details in *The Origins of Totalitarianism*, that Arendt sets out to rethink politics, and with it the human condition, such that this will become the focus and title of her book *The Human Condition*. The Greek world, to which she continuously turns her attention, is first and foremost an imaginary model upon which she projects her reflections, that is, a laboratory of thought for uncovering a pure concept of politics that stands in direct opposition to the abyss of totalitarian dehumanization, and thus to the long political tradition, itself originating in Greece, that did not prevent the West from falling into this abyss.

As mentioned above, Arendt also traces back to Greek antiquity the philosophical tradition that conceives of politics as the struggle for power or the choice of the best regime of rule, aimed at imposing order and stability. Although marked by certain variations, this is the tradition that reaches up to the present and that still permeates our political language, despite having been pushed to the very brink, during the middle of the last century, of the totalitarian abyss. Against Plato and the tradition he inaugurated, Arendt brings the accusation of having essentially obscured the genuine experience of the polis, rooted in the human condition of plurality, replacing it with a notion of politics conceived as the procedure for governing people and administering their affairs. To be free in the polis, Arendt never tires of repeating, meant both "to be free from the inequality present in rulership and to move in a sphere where neither rule nor being ruled existed."[16] In other words, it meant conceiving of politics in terms of an experience that was participatory and plural, completely incompatible with a model of vertical, hierarchical organization of command, be it by one person, by a few, or by many, according to the classic typology of forms of government that we call monarchy, oligarchy, and democracy. Or, even worse, be it the command of the master over women and slaves in the domestic sphere.

With the tradition inaugurated by Plato, Arendt maintains, the original idea of politics, along with the experience of the polis that had engendered it, disappeared from the world of "human affairs" and was replaced and superseded by political doctrines focused upon governing and ruling. Crucially, however, it did not disappear entirely, according to Arendt, but survived as "a hidden treasure" ready to be "rediscovered" at certain favorable moments, which, in modern history, most notably include various revolutionary events. In contrast to canonical interpretations, Arendt argues that, in fact, one of the most important aspects of the revolutions of the eighteenth century, and especially of the American Revolution, was the rediscovery of the political experience of plural interaction within a public, shared space. The history of revolution, "which politically spells out the innermost story of the modern age," writes Arendt, "could be told in parable form as the tale of an age-old treasure which, under the most varied circumstances, appears abruptly, unexpectedly, and disappears again, under different mysterious conditions, as though it were a fata morgana."[17] Arendt argues that although the revolutionary events were triggered by the violent, insurrectional movements characteristic of the process of *liberation*, yet what the revolutionaries of the eighteenth century rediscovered, through their encounters in assemblies and other shared spaces of action, was the ancient taste for *freedom*. She does not hesitate to underline how "conspicuous by its absence . . . was the deep concern with forms of government so characteristic of the American Revolution, but also very important in the initial stages of the French Revolution."[18] Moreover, she notes that the rediscovery of politics on the part of revolutionaries, as a type of renewed political paradigm, was something that occurred in the centuries that followed. This came about, as Simona Forti explains, by

1: The Idea of Democracy

means of subsequent "epiphanies that leave their mark on the development of modern states, or that survive at their margins." These include, among others, the Paris Commune of 1871, the Russian Revolution of 1917, the German democracy of Workers' Councils in 1918, the Hungarian Revolution, and the American civil disobedience movement of the 1960s.[19] If there exists a nexus, entirely modern, linking the rediscovery of politics to revolution, it reappears at some of the most significant and, so to speak, structurally important moments of insurrection, resistance, and protest within the modern era.

That an enthusiastic scholar of Arendt like Miguel Abensour should speak of "democracy against the state" and propose the category of "insurgent democracy" should therefore come as no surprise. One suspects, however, that the image of a democracy in perennial effervescence, at the heart of which would be "the fraternal disorder in opposition to the power of the leaders: in sum, non-domination, a non-restrictive and egalitarian political bond in opposition to order,"[20] has its limits in regards to its adaptability to an Arendtian vision of politics. And, more importantly, the suspicion remains that the clear distinction, established by Arendt, between the usually violent movement inherent to the process of liberation and the completely nonviolent character of the experience of freedom is one that cannot be dismissed so easily. It is worth recalling that, according to Arendt, "politically speaking, it is sufficient to say that power and violence are not the same. Power and violence are opposite," and they are so completely opposed that "to speak of non-violent power is actually redundant."[21] "Power corresponds to the human ability not just to act but to act in concert. Power is never the property of an individual; it belongs to a group and remains in existence only so long as the group keeps together."[22] Put another way, political power is neither the residue nor the product of the potential movement of insurgency, but rather it is immanent to the shared space of its actualization, coextensive with its interactive plural source. To put it even more directly, Arendt does not at all interpret power in terms of struggle, or even in terms of conflict and opposition. Hers is not a model that is *against* a particular form of government, which obviously exhibits its most extreme degeneration in the totalitarian regime. Hers is rather a model that is *alternative* to a politics modeled upon governing, another idea of politics with respect to that founded upon governing and ruling, against which it can resist but not in any constitutive or, so to speak, vitally subversive sense. This means that the dimension of insurgency, with the various forms of struggle and violence that the revolutionary imaginary includes, is decidedly outside the framework that Arendt reserves for the pure concept of politics. Hers is a framework that not only finds it hard to include the notion of "insurgent democracy" proposed by Abensour, but decidedly rejects any vision of the "insurgent multitudes," so often invoked today, whose epochal task would consist of destroying the global imperial order.[23]

The issue is crucial because it allows us to highlight how the frequent connection to Arendt on the part of the authors who are currently engaged in radicalizing the idea of democracy is often marked by a fundamental ambiguity that fails to do justice to the originality of her political thought. Emblematic, in this sense, is Claude Lefort's position. On the one hand, Lefort, echoing a classically Arendtian theme, contrasts "democratic invention" with "totalitarian domination," interpreting democracy as the "savage" revolutionary nucleus of politics "that lives by a continual interrogation of its own premises and that betrays itself the moment it is definitively organized into a political system."[24] On the other hand, he insists on defining democracy itself as a "regime of indetermination" that, by revitalizing the primary division between those who want to dominate and those who do not want to be dominated, between the oppressors and the oppressed, continually reactivates this conflict, which thus becomes an inexhaustible source of disorder and libertarian effervescence. Lefort's distance from Arendt is evident in the accent he places upon democracy as permanent contestation, as a perennial and indomitable field of struggle and demands.[25]

In some respects, even if never explicitly, Jacques Rancière's "anarchic democracy" seems to be closer to the Arendtian framework. Taking to the extreme the principle of the absence of government (*archè*), Rancière identifies democracy with the scandalous concept of "government of anybody and everybody," exemplified by the way in which, in democratic Athens, rulers and offices were chosen at random through selection by lot, with lot being itself the proper political procedure for a people of equals.[26] Like Arendt, Rancière severely critiques Plato, seeing already at work within the great philosopher, creator of a political model entrusting rule to an oligarchy of experts, that elite hatred of democracy which hints at "the intolerable egalitarian condition of inequality," that is, a hatred for that "primary indistinction between governors and governed" which constitutes, for Rancière, the indispensable, and indeed unbearable, foundation of the political.[27] Rather than being interested in democracy as a shared space of interaction, therefore, Rancière is interested in the absolute egalitarianism that the idea of democracy can inspire. Rather than in interactive plurality, as the condition and source of power shared by actors who are equal but distinct, he is interested in a critical and subversive use of the category of equality, which he posits as originary and foundational, as a "claim of radical horizontality."[28] Insurgency and equality, however, all the more if understood as constitutive elements of the political, are, for that matter and clearly, Marxian categories rather than Arendtian ones. Reconciling Marx with Arendt is an extremely arduous endeavor, all the more so if we take into account the complicated critical interpretation that Arendt devotes to Marx.[29] Although many of the authors mentioned above have taken up this very challenge, the revolutionary and egalitarian grammar they employ is fundamentally incompatible with the Arendtian concept of politics. Or, if one prefers, it highlights the boundary between Arendt's concept and their own. Suffice it to mention the particular emphasis these authors put upon justice and social equality, as well as insurgent masses and emancipatory struggle, to say nothing of the accent on perennial protest or "creative violence" that redeems the oppressed.

Yet Arendt's insistence on the plural source of power—which engenders, nourishes, and delimits the space of interaction, and which she characterizes as absolutely nonviolent—continues to appear today as an indispensable element for the task of addressing the issue of democracy in a fresh way. Just as seemingly indispensable appears her emphasis upon the "faculty of freedom itself" as the source "which animates and inspires all human activity,"[30] a source that finds its place of regeneration precisely in the sphere of political interaction. Revisiting the Arendtian idea of politics with a certain unprejudiced eye, we might thus call it "surging democracy."

There are good reasons for proposing this expression in preference to others. While the concept of "insurgent democracy" evokes wild, vital, and effervescent energies, which tend to find their expression through conflict and antagonistic struggle, the concept of "surging democracy" has the completely Arendtian virtue of highlighting the generative rather than the oppositional aspect of plural interaction. One could simply say that the term surging democracy avoids substantiating democracy, first and foremost, in its being *against*, choosing instead to present its core as essentially affirmative rather than negative. Actually, surging democracy draws from a political imaginary which is alternative, not only in respect to the model of rulership, but also in respect to that political imaginary, mentioned above, that understands democracy as "movement" and "field of struggle," the arena of a vital, subversive, and oppositional negativity. Besides, it is worth noting that, as Abensour acknowledges, the term *insurgency* is closely tied, and not just etymologically, to the term *insurrection*.[31] The etymon that they both share can be traced back to the Latin verb *surgere*, which, in its form *insurgere*, accentuates the notion of "rising up against," "standing up against": from which we derive the conventional meaning, found in dictionaries, of "insurrection" as "armed uprising." However, the verb *surgere* has another meaning far less vertical or bellicose in nature: that of "springing forth," "coming into existence," as is said, for instance, in regard to the "source" of a river. Or when something is said to be "welling up" because it springs forth, emerges, pours out.

In revisiting the Arendtian idea of politics, the term surging is intended to express these various connotations, accentuating the experience of democracy in its germinal, birthing state. It is a state that is likewise generative, incipient and spontaneous, nascent. It is as if this nascent state, this generative and creative phase of the political, were at the origin of the very idea of democracy. Or as if surging democracy were the conceptual basis for evaluating the various forms of political action to which we apply the name democracy.

Tellingly, revisiting the Arendtian idea of politics in order to reconfigure it as surging democracy is an undertaking that turns out to be particularly congruent with Arendt's own critical approach to modern democracy, which, according to her, has the fault of being focused upon social questions. Suffice it to say that the pure form of politics, to which she appeals, relegates to the private sphere the subject of work along with all concerns inherent to it, *in primis* everything tied to the necessities of biological life. It is precisely in these terms that Arendt frames her critical reading of Marx, accusing him of having glorified work (*labor*), thus making it the foundation of politics.[32] And it is in roughly similar terms that Arendt critiques liberalism, whose philosophy, according to her, is blameworthy first and foremost for claiming that politics "must be concerned almost exclusively with the maintenance of life and the safeguarding of its interests," that is, must take care of "the gigantic and still increasing sphere of social and economic life whose administration has overshadowed the political realm ever since the beginning of the modern age."[33] Readers of Arendt must get used to her anomalous, original, and problematic approach: coming to terms with her means coming to terms with her pure and, in a certain sense, untimely definition of the political. Political power, far from being a means, according to her, is an end itself, and exists only in its actualization. Put another way, Arendt decidedly gives to the political sphere an autonomous status, distinguishing the domain of the "political" from that of the "social" and, even more so, from that of the "economic." From this can be deduced the great distance separating her from a Marxist vision as much as from a liberal or neoliberal one.

This would further explain, according to Sheldom Wolin, the Arendtian wariness of the term democracy: not only because, in the modern age, as Wolin recalls, "the impulse of democracy has been to override that distinction," but also because "historically, democracy has been the means by which the many have sought access to political power in the hope that it could be used to redress their economic and social lot."[34] In other words, the "social question," the aspiration to free oneself from poverty and a state of need, is inscribed in the egalitarian vocabulary that has shaped the modern history of democracy. All the more conspicuous, then, is Arendt's obstinacy in removing the social question from the public sphere in order to recuperate a pure concept of the political. Her understanding of "politics" is definitively anomalous and original. Precisely for this reason, but not for this reason alone, it has often been criticized and deemed difficult to work with.

It has been observed that Arendt's thought is largely based upon a utopian vision of the polis and that her notion of politics has unrealistic traits. That which Arendt seems to have no interest in accounting for, writes Pier Paolo Portinaro, "is the sense of conflict that inevitably accompanies the condition of plurality, and which in the end is the cause of slippage between a principle of action and a model of government, which she interprets simply in terms of political degeneration or alienation from the realm of politics."[35] In truth, when she reflects upon the Greek world that she takes as a model, Arendt never fails to point out the agonism that characterized it; on the contrary, she highlights it. Her emphasis, however, is on the contest between peers as a manifestation of the agonistic spirit, as a means of excelling and distinguishing oneself; it is not upon the conflict, even violent conflict, that would be the substance and the driver of the political or, so to speak, its constitutive principle. Certainly, to declare, as Arendt does, that violence and political power are incompatible phenomena, and to deny that conflict and hostility are the foundation of politics, can only result in a theoretical gesture that is hardly realistic when compared to the traditional canons of political realism. Yet, elaborated as it is—not by chance—in the aftermath of the totalitarian catastrophe, the "utopian" impulse of the Arendtian perspective stands out, even today, as an element of great interest for those looking to rethink politics in nonviolent and affirmative terms, that is, those looking to conceive of it as something beyond, not only the ferocity it historically often displays, but also beyond the cynical standpoint of certain intellectual attitudes that assume this ferocity as an insurmountable and basic political mark. Although few others have reflected upon human violence and the unprecedented manifestations of this violence as she has, Arendt does not espouse any metaphysics of force, nor does she make conflict an agent for constructing political systems of order aimed at disciplining the outcomes of this very conflict. On the contrary, she denounces the tragic complicity with the human history of destruction of certain political theories that—from Hobbes to Weber and beyond—equated political power with the organization of violence. And she rebukes the general consensus "among political theorists from Left to Right that violence is nothing more than the most flagrant manifestation of power."[36]

Those searching Arendt's texts for the detached cynicism of realism will find there the enthralling *pathos* of utopia. They will find a philosophical imaginary filled with hope for "human affairs" that refuses to idolize the destructiveness of critique and dares to speak of the political experience within a shared public space as one of happiness.

2 Plurality

IN RECENT YEARS, following the rise of right-wing populism in Europe and the United States, Arendt's *The Origins of Totalitarianism* has seen an exceptional increase in sales.¹ As Zoe Williams, in February 2017, pointed out in *The Guardian*, "commentators have been referencing the work since Donald Trump's election in November but rarely has this spurred so many people to actually buy a copy."² Yet when interviewed in the same article, excellent Arendtian scholar Griselda Pollock rightly suggested that, in light of the current populist turn of western liberal democracies, our interest in Arendt's texts should instead focus on *The Human Condition*. This is especially true for the phenomenon known as "digital populism," a recent form of populism characterized by the use of social media.

The difficulty of giving a precise definition of populism is well known. This is evident in the numerous studies dedicated to the subject. In general, however, a common feature we can identify is the belief that the people are endowed with an authentic moral integrity, whereas political parties and professional politicians, interested only in power and personal profit, are seen as irredeemably corrupt. From this come the constant appeals on the part of populist leaders to the "virtuousness" of the people in contrast to the "evils" of the political establishment or, as we say, the clique of party elites. Another prominent characteristic is the populist mindset's tendency to embrace the values and political culture of the Right: these include (referring only to recent times) nationalist, identitarian, and sovereignist attitudes, which feed on anti-immigrant discourses as well as xenophobic, homophobic, and sexist sentiment.[3] In this regard, the expression "exclusive neopopulism" has been coined as different and distinct from "inclusive neopopulism," the latter understood as a form of populism that, far from insisting on identitarian themes, includes within the concept of "the people," immigrants and other typical "enemies" of exclusive neopopulism.[4] On the other hand, it is well known that "ideological and programmatic flexibility is one of the defining characteristics of neopopulism," qualities that lend it a "chameleon-like nature":[5] far from being a firm principle, the inclusive attitude, due to a variety of changes in strategy or shifting government alliances, has no difficulty fading away, even turning into its opposite at times. Indeed, it is hard to contain the universe of various populisms existing today within a clear framework of distinctive classifications, including the elementary distinction between Right and Left.[6] The fact remains, however, that digital populism, in its most explicit form, which celebrates the virtual communicative environment as the substance and foundation of the political, maintains a specific profile: especially in regards to so-called *e-democracy,* that is, a direct democracy online, from which digital populism claims to spring forth as political movement, and whose fullest realization it aspires to achieve, through the "overcoming" of representative democracy, even on the institutional level.

A specific example of digital populism can be found in Italy, where the Five Star Movement, which ascended to power with The Lega in June 2018, wasted no time in reaffirming the necessity of going beyond representative democracy in order to let the people rule directly. By reformatting the traditional populist topic of direct democracy versus representative democracy, and by addressing "the generic internet user as the new prototype of the 'common man' of populism," digital populism puts a particular emphasis on the networked participatory form of politics it claims to enact, that is, a form of disintermediate and horizontal interconnection, which also functions as a means for permanent consultation and that presents itself as "true" and even "absolute" direct democracy.[7] However, within the Five Star Movement's organizational structure, which functions via a digital platform called not coincidentally the "Rousseau platform," this horizontality entails not only a direct connection, in real time, between the people and the political leader, who thus becomes the spokesperson in regards to the general will, but also a more disturbing decisional power on the part of the president and webmaster of this same platform. The alleged horizontality, proclaimed in the slogan "everyone counts as one," is thus severely undermined.

Beyond this and other notable complications, what resurfaces in contemporary populist jargon, in any case, is the old rhetoric of "the will of the people," readjusted to the new figure of the "people of the web," along with the immediate connection, via Twitter, Facebook, or Instagram, between the people and the leader. In fact, the leader assumes a particular role here, since digital populism aspires to legislate in a way that no longer relies upon parliamentary procedure but rather upon social media and blogs. The traditional antiparliamentarism of the Right thus finds a new means of engagement. As Alessandro Dal Lago observes, digital populism, by exhuming a typical characteristic of "Peronism," demonstrates a peculiar tendency to encourage the coexistence of "political issues of the Right and the Left," within an ideology in which identitarian attitudes, hostile to immigrants and the Romani, as well as, more generally, to cosmopolitanism, commingle with efforts to support the poor and marginalized, the retired and unemployed, by means of a redistribution of wealth.[8] This ideological flexibility, linked to a certain "chameleon-like ability,"[9] indeed produces its fruits. Tellingly, recent history, especially in Italy, provides ample evidence of how, on the one hand, digital populists do not hold back from allying with the authoritarian populisms of the sovereigntist Right, and how, on the other hand, populist leaders are particularly effective at exploiting the propagandistic and manipulative potential of the internet. To the extent that speaking of populism or neopopulism remains challenging, it is because, in the age of social media, the numerous existing forms of populism all tend to blend together.

It is nonetheless easy to see how, despite the continual emphasis upon the people, understood as an organic unity and the expression of a homogenous will (manifested through majority vote but that justifies the purging of dissenters), it is the concept of the individual that resurfaces here, adapting itself to the new authoritarian context. Individualism, reformatted in networked version, and demagogic neo-authoritarianism go together seamlessly. On one hand, the atomized individual of modernity is resuscitated in new form, and incorporates itself into the model of the so-called "networked individualism," that is, the very model that, according to the claims of digital populism, is the constitutive element of e-democracy as authentic direct democracy. On the other hand, the authoritarian-minded populist leader, exploiting the disintermediate connection with "followers" or "friends," finds in internet users fertile ground for manipulation and the dissemination of disinformation.[10] The populist leader of today has, moreover, a variety of ways of updating, via the web, the well-known mimetic strategy that makes of him the "common man" of the people. Through political or media pronouncements, and posturing as the people's spokesperson, he even adopts the visceral language of the mob and openly espouses intolerance. Described by some critics as neoplebs,[11] the people are kept in a state of constant excitement. This is due both to the uninterrupted flow of communication from the leader, who mirrors back and plays upon the people's emotions, and to the stimulating effects of so-called instant democracy, which, by means of constant polling and online feedback, creates a climate of permanent electoral campaign. In hindsight, we could say that the virtuous marriage of democracy and the internet—which was discussed so optimistically only a short time ago—has disappointed expectations, ultimately giving birth to a dangerous progeny that combines an emphasis on networked participatory culture, a revival of authoritarianism, and a nurturing of the typical populist fruits of resentment and anger.

In *The Origins of Totalitarianism* Arendt offers indeed precious insights for understanding how these fruits, nurtured and paired with a "self-centered bitterness,"[12] take root, ripen, and thrive. For this and numerous other reasons, her masterpiece on totalitarianism deserves all the attention it is receiving from readers today. Yet for an even more valuable study bearing upon the present situation and its problems, one might look to Arendt's work *The Human Condition*, in which she engages with the issue of interactive political participation and, even if she never mentions it by name, she ponders on direct democracy and reframes its concept in ways that radically and, so to speak, preventively contrast the very notion of direct democracy that digital populism is proposing today in online form. It is worth recalling that, in *The Human Condition*, the word *democracy* is mentioned only in passing and

2: Plurality

never qualified with the adjective *direct*. Although Arendt's definition of politics in terms of a plurality of human beings acting in concert in a shared public space is explicitly modeled on that democracy of the ancient polis which modern political vocabulary qualifies as direct, she avoids engaging with any type of lexical distinction in reference to specific forms of government. Arendt prefers to articulate her thought on the "pure concept of what constitute the political" by means of an innovative—and indeed anomalous—vocabulary that intentionally leaves aside traditional terminology and conceptuality. This is evident in the fact that one of the central categories of *The Human Condition* is natality, a term entirely absent within traditional political lexicon, which instead willingly engages with the belligerent topic of death. Yet more evidence lies in the fact that in the political space of appearance she depicts, there are no individuals or citizens, but unique human beings and actors; neither is there "the people," but "plurality." Margaret Canovan has rightly stressed that Arendt "'augmented' the world by one word: the word plurality," adding that "the most fruitful way of reading her political thought is to treat her analysis of modernity as a context for the interesting things she has to say about the fact that politics goes among plural persons with space between."[13]

Arendt's commitment to the category of plurality manifests itself in her writings of the early 1950s and reaches its peak, at the end of the decade, in *The Human Condition*. One could even trace a speculative thread that goes from her initial focus on the issue of plurality of opinions—the *dokei moi*, the "it appears to me," that attests for the plurality of *doxai* (opinions) and has its model in Socrates's *politeuein*[14]—to her final choice of giving plurality an ontological status as *the* specific characteristic of the human condition. Crucially, this status calls on bodily appearance as it is first displayed at the moment of birth and whenever we appear to others in our physical uniqueness. Based on the fact that "nobody is ever the same as anyone else who ever lived, lives, or will live," Arendt writes, "human plurality is the paradoxical plurality of unique beings," a condition already physically disclosed by the uniqueness of every newborn, that is, by "the fact of natality, in which the faculty of action is ontologically rooted."[15] It is worth lingering here on the difference, if not the incompatibility, between her initial interest in the plurality of opinions and her final understanding of human plurality as the fundamental condition of politics. If the first allows for a political interpretation of Arendt based on dialogue, negotiation, and communicative action, the second presents us with a radical ontological refoundation of politics, which puts profoundly into question the average model of direct democracy and especially the current digital version of this very model.

Arendt's insistence on the spatial, physical, and corporeal dimension of political interaction cannot be stressed enough. Politics, as she defines it, is a public space of appearance in which human beings, through their interactions with others, distinguish and reveal themselves. It is a physical space of reciprocal appearance in which those present see and are seen, hear and are heard. Arendt writes that "with word and deed we insert ourselves into the human world, and this insertion is like a second birth, in which we confirm and take upon ourselves the naked fact of our original physical appearance."[16] Nothing could be farther from the individualistic ontology of modernity and, even more so, from its current metamorphosis into the digital individualism that addresses the general internet user. Arendt proposes a participatory conception of politics that calls for an active, performative distinction of a plurality of physically present actors, flesh-and-blood human beings. As Judith Butler rightly points out, "for Arendt, political action takes place on the condition that the body appear. I appear to others, and they appear to me, which means that some space between us allows each to appear."[17] What is striking, in Arendt's idea of the political, is the stress on spatial proximity—if not the "face-to-face" physical contiguity—of an interactive bodily plurality. Her original and indeed radical version of direct democracy, if we want to persist in using this expression, entails a space that is physically shared, in which those present appear to each other, through words and deeds, and in so doing exhibit their uniqueness and their capacity to begin new things, the two characteristics already apparent in each newborn. Put another way, through interaction in a shared space, the plurality of embodied uniqueness—on display not only in each newborn but also daily within every human being, "in the unique shape of the body and sound of the voice"[18]—acquires a political status that confirms the corporeal materiality of the entire Arendtian narrative about politics.

In highlighting the materiality of this interactive space of appearance, Arendt pushes her argument to its extremes. She suggests, in fact, that those who are present and who speak are not political actors because of what they say, but because they say it to others, who share, in bodily terms, this interactive space of reciprocal exposure through acts and deeds. To formulate it differently, paradoxical as it may seem, Arendt is first and foremost interested in the concrete relationality of embodied political actors, not in the contents of their discourse, nor, as one says today, in their political agenda. As if the basic criteria, for endorsing or rejecting certain "contents" of the political agenda, were inherent to the plural dimension of relationality itself and the issues it entails—equal ontological dignity for each unique human being, equal freedom and equal risk in expressing and embracing this uniqueness, common responsibility in opening up and preserving political spaces for interaction. Arendt does not, however, conceive this acting in concert as a means for actualizing specific political contents, but rather as an experience that contains within itself its own end; it is a distinctive experience whose end is precisely to actively express the human condition of plurality.

If it is indeed possible to consider Arendt's political thought as a valuable resource for thematizing the democratic principles of freedom and equality, it is nonetheless important to recognize that, in her anomalous conception of politics, they do not work as principles or ideals but rather as *modes* of acting in concert. To put it in simple terms, for Arendt, *outside* the political space there can be no free and equal human beings who, making this freedom and equality into a principle to be claimed, would then introduce it into the sphere of politics as a democratic instance. On the contrary, it is the experience of interaction within a public space that makes political actors equal, allowing them to discover and experience freedom in the shared space of its actualization. Arendt, referring as usual to the original political experience of the Greeks, writes: "neither equality nor freedom was understood as a quality inherent in human nature, they were both not *physei*, given by nature and growing out by themselves; they were *nomo*, that is, conventional and artificial, the product of human effort and qualities of the man-made world."[19] It is precisely politics that makes human actors free and equal. In regards to the category of equality—so central to the concept of democracy in all of the versions that the modern age provides—it is important to realize, as Claude Lefort points out, that far from being an end in itself, for Arendt, equality is instead an invention; "it is an effect or simply a sign of the moment which raises men above life and opens up to a *common world*."[20] According to her idea of politics as space for interaction, "it is by participating in this space, by acceding to the *visibility* of a public stage that men define and apprehend one another as equals."[21] This means that in her vision, equality and freedom are not principles—self-evident natural rights, as it were—which precede politics and which politics must either conform to or seek to bring about within society. Rather they are modes of interacting with others, inherent to political experience itself. Politics, in Arendtian terms, is politics in the authentic sense, first and foremost, because of its modes of actualization, and only secondly, because of the contents that, in coherence with these modes, it may inspire.

Many critics have noted that, precisely because Arendt insists on the performative aspect of political participation to the detriment of political contents, her position appears not only unrealistic but also ineffectual on a practical level. After all, getting back to our initial topic, what could Arendt oppose to populist ideology? Yet, upon closer examination, her insistence on a material and embodied form of relationality as *the* constitutive element of politics—and, more precisely, of a politics understood as the direct, interactive participation of a plurality of actors—possesses considerable critical potential for challenging the model of absolute democracy invoked by digital populism. The principal point of contrast, simple as it may seem, obviously has to do with the deliberate absence of bodies or of corporeal relationships within this supposedly absolute democracy. While Arendt rejects the individualistic ontology of the modern political tradition, replacing its abstract, atomized subject with an embodied and relational subjectivity, supporters of digital populism transform this same subject into an even further isolated and—literally—remote individual. Not coincidentally, this individual is situated in the isolation of what Arendt calls the private realm. The virtual *agorà* functions precisely as an immaterial network connecting private individuals, who remain so private and isolated that their presence in the virtual political space presupposes their physical absence. As Arendt might say, today we are confronted with the disconcerting phenomenon of unrelated individuals, hidden in the obscurity of the private realm, who invade the digital public sphere and are thus touted as the ideal actors of direct democracy.

2: Plurality

Reflecting on this phenomenon, scholars have often concentrated upon the manipulative aspects inherent to the social media universe, notoriously dominated by the proliferation of fake news and "alternative facts" that generate conspiracy theories and multiply opportunities for hate speech. In the so-called post-truth era—revealingly inclined to war-related metaphors—"cyberwarfare," by means of "armies of trolls" and "weaponized disinformation," makes use of ever more sophisticated algorithms to manufacture ideological consent. What prevails is "a hypersimplified, sensationalist, and titillating form of communication, modeled upon that of advertising, and addressed to a loyal audience looking for confirmation of what it already believes."[22] The isolated individual who participates in the virtual *agorà* is a digital product as well, at least to the extent that this isolation—or the lack of a common world that, like a table, as Arendt says, "relates and separates men at the same time"[23]—makes the internet user particularly vulnerable to manipulation. That this manipulation tends to whip up the emotional energies of the online masses and to redirect them toward aggressive and conspiratorial forms of expression is too well-known a phenomenon to need any further explanation. In short, by exploiting the self-centered bitterness of its users, social media are notoriously "apt at communicating slogans, abuse, ridicule, extraordinary promises and claims, but entirely unfit for accommodating reasonable exchange."[24] Hate speech regularly commingles with fear of difference, be it racial, cultural, religious, sexual, or gendered. Nothing new, in this regard, in respect to the ideological playbook of the different right-wing political camps, including its ultrareactionary and parafascistic elements. What is new, however, is the appeal to e-democracy on the part of digital populists, an appeal that, when it mentions the "people" or "the will of the people," does not intend the fascist masses but rather, paradoxically, those free and autonomous individuals who manifest their freedom of speech by participating in the virtual *agorà* on the basis of an equal access. Phantasmatic replica of the autonomous subject of liberal doctrines, the free and equal individual resurfaces as the fundamental "value" of digital populism. In this sense, one could even say that digital populism seemingly discovers the "solution" to an age-old problem: while direct democracy worked well for the ancient polis, it is not applicable to the modern state, whose dimensions require a representative form of democracy. Yet by exploiting the internet's recent evolution in personal devices connecting everyone to everyone, digital populism not only makes direct democracy possible but, theoretically, makes it possible on a global scale. Of course, within this potential global scenario, bodies are called upon neither to move about nor to share an actual physical space. At most, a certain role is reserved for the hands and eyes, or for whatever other body parts can help in connecting to the internet.

It may be noted that there are disturbing similarities between the populist emphasis on digital democracy as an "overcoming" or "vanquishing" of representative democracy and Arendt's own critical stance in regard to representative democracy. In fact, plurality, as Arendt intends it, requires a space of appearance and is intolerant of any mechanism of representation. Given that it is made up of unique human beings who, acting in concert, engender a material, relational space in order to actively and mutually disclose *who* they are, plurality is un-representable. To sum up, what is at stake, in Arendt's conception of politics, is the physical presence of a plurality that cannot be re-presented in its absence.

In *On Revolution*, Arendt criticizes representative democracy for its effect of depoliticizing citizens by reducing them to voters who "act" only on the day of elections. This is, uncoincidentally, the same text in which Arendt declares that "the great good fortune of the America Revolution" was that it took place in a country already "organized in self-governing bodies." It was a country divided up into various civic political bodies—into districts, counties, and townships— created by the newly arrived British immigrants as a direct and participatory means of self-governance. Arendt is quick to point out, however, that these bodies "were not conceived as governments, strictly speaking; they did not imply rule and the division of the people into rulers and ruled." They consisted rather "in the formation of a political realm that enjoyed power and was entitled to claim rights without possessing or claiming sovereignty."[25] For Arendt, the great good fortune of the American Revolution was to have emerged in a country that already conceived of political power in participatory terms and, even more so, that had distributed this experience across a wide range of local political spaces. It is precisely this form of political organization, built upon a diffuse network of political spaces rather than on the centralized mechanism of representation, that Arendt draws upon when she declares her preference for republicanism and the council system. These are, in fact, institutional models that, instead of making the transmission of power vertical, guarantee citizens spaces of public freedom in which they can interact, that is, spaces of "participatory democracy."[26] In *On Violence*, Arendt describes, on more than one occasion, republicanism and federalism as desirable alternatives to the nation-state. In doing so, she affirms that "the American government," even though it unfortunately entered into the European heritage of the sovereign nation-state "as though it were its patrimony," has the merit of being "based on a great plurality of powers and their mutual checks and balances."[27] In this text, Arendt goes so far as to claim that "all political institutions are manifestations of power," that is, "government is essentially organized and institutionalized power."[28] For Arendt, this means that political institutions do not create power but rather are sustained by it and ideally called upon to organize power by distributing its regeneration across plural spaces of interaction.

In *The Human Condition*, however, Arendt's approach to the question of politics is more of a speculative vein and avoids getting bogged down in institutional issues. For Arendt in the theoretical context of *The Human Condition*, moreover, it is not a matter of adapting the ancient model of direct democracy to the conditions of modern democracy, but rather of recovering, after the catastrophe of totalitarianism, as Simona Forti duly notes, "the original meaning, progressively lost over time, of the term politics,"[29] or, in other words, "the pure concept of what constitutes the political."[30]

Anyhow, Arendt's distance from the paradigm of the modern nation-state, conceived of in territorial and sovereign terms, comes across in *The Human Condition*, too, when she argues that politics, although consisting of the interaction of a physical plurality, does not need a territory, much less a territory whose borders delimit the sovereignty of the state. "Wherever you go, you will be a polis," claims a famous line of Thucydides that Arendt quotes and endorses in order to argue that the space of politics exists "between people living together for this purpose, no matter where they happen to be."[31] Politics, in her view, is a relational space that comes into being with the event of plural interaction and, together with it, disappears. It is contingent and intermittent, a political experience of plurality, generated by human beings whenever and wherever they act in concert, capable of lasting as long as their actions and whose form can neither be encapsulated in any system nor bound to any territory. Instead of direct democracy, we could therefore speak of a phenomenology of the political focused upon the birthing moment of democracy itself. It is a moment both germinal and germinative that, while linked to certain circumstances, can spring up, surging anywhere. After all, given Arendt's firm opposition to the territorial, nationalist, and centralized characteristics of the nation-state, it is not by chance that we venture, here, to call "surging democracy" the very political scenario to which she gives instead the anomalous name of "space of appearance."

The space of appearance, Arendt points out:

> comes into being wherever men are together in the manner of speech and action, and therefore predates and precedes all formal constitution of the public realm and the various forms of government, that is, the various forms in which the public realm can be organized. . . . Its peculiarity is that it does not survive the actuality of the movement which brought it into being, but disappears not only with the dispersal of men—as in the case of great catastrophes when the body politic of a people is destroyed—but with the disappearance or arrest of the activities themselves. Wherever people gather together, it is potentially there, but only potentially, not necessarily and not forever.[32]

Put another way, the space of appearance can neither be guaranteed nor preserved beyond its enactment: politics, as Arendt intends it, is an intermittent event that evokes the form of a surging democracy always in the making, whose nascent status is produced and reproduced, every time anew, by the interactions of different concrete pluralities. It is worth noting that at center stage in these interacting pluralities is the reciprocal exhibition of *who* each actor is (as a unique and irreplaceable human being), while *what* the actors are, that is, their social and cultural identities, is not given any constitutive role. Arendt's accent on uniqueness as the absolute difference of everybody from everybody else—that is, the same embodied uniqueness plurality consists of—goes together with her coherent aversion for any form of politics constructed on collective identities, be it in relation to national, ethnic, cultural, social, or, in the worst case, racial differences.

2: Plurality

A decisive and perhaps underappreciated aspect of Arendt's political thought is that plurality, by functioning as an antidote to the homogeneity of the people, the nation, or the race, does succeed in neutralizing the inevitable mechanisms of expulsion and exclusion that identity-frames risk begetting and empowering, and which populist demagogues, especially in the digital era, know how to exploit emotionally, if not to produce. In fact, social media is clearly not just the new technological *means* by which the populist reserve of anger and hatred toward "the identity of the other" is disseminated and offered up to demagogues' manipulation; it is rather the primary setting in which this anger and hatred are generated, organized, and intensified. All the more reason therefore to reflect, along with Arendt, on the concept of plurality nowadays. To put it differently, exclusive populist agendas constructed on nationalism, xenophobia, racism, sexism, homophobia, and the like, are highly incompatible with Arendt's idea of politics. In her terms, interactive plurality demands and structurally consists of inclusion: not inclusion in a "people" but rather in a horizontal space of interaction between unique and equal human actors. Its limit is the material dimension of the shared space that comes from physical proximity. Openness toward others, regardless of their belonging to a group, a nation, a minority, a religion or to whatever identitarian frame, is its content.

Rereading *The Human Condition*, with a certain glibness, one could argue that Arendt outlines a political scenario that is situationist, spontaneous, or even "ludic" in nature.[33] Or, at the very least, that she allows for a perspective in which what matters is the *event*, as the public, highly visible interaction of a plurality of human actors, while no attention is paid to the array of motivations, needs, demands, ideas, and even identity issues, which drove these actors to assemble and take action in the first place. The explicit choice, on the part of Arendt, to employ theatrical terminology, calling those who act in concert "actors" and describing the interactive space as a scene of reciprocal appearance in which everyone is both actor and spectator, seems to make this interpretation plausible. Moreover, Arendt shows a keen appreciation for the Aristotelian notion of "drama" as the artistic imitation of action (from the Greek verb *dran*, "to act"), declaring that "the theatre is the political art par excellence; only there is the political sphere of human life transposed into art."[34]

In order to avoid nudging Arendt's political thought into an aestheticizing framework that ill suits it, however, we should add a few clarifications. Arendt's insistence on the spatial dimension that enables actors to see and be seen, hear and be heard, concerns only actors themselves rather than any potential external observers who might enjoy this "performance" as it were a "spectacle." What is indeed spectacular, for Arendt, are the movements of people in large crowds of revolutions, which, like in the French Revolution, sweeping up the impoverished and destitute masses to burst like a "torrent" onto the stage of history, continue to capture the western political imaginary. Unfortunately, in fact, as Arendt laments, the authentic heritage of the eighteenth-century revolutions, which for her consisted of the rediscovery of political freedom as acting in concert, has been obscured by the dramatic imagery of crowds in revolt. Of course, as her dense analysis of the phenomenon of revolution testifies, Arendt is conscious of the motives and ideals that incite people to act and rebel. Indeed, she is well aware that the public experience of freedom, rediscovered as a "hidden treasure" by modern revolutionaries, is preceded by a movement of *liberation* from the yoke of regimes felt as unjust and despotic or from intolerable social conditions of inequality and poverty. She does not, in fact, deny that the rediscovery of public freedom was preceded and even caused by a set of motivations and claims whose insurrectional, propelling force, regularly throughout history, turns into violence. She does, however, deny that the substance of this political experience, rediscovered at the time of revolutions, consists of these motivations and claims. For Arendt, the struggle, even violent struggle, against domination in the name of principles and demands, which revolutionaries feel to be urgent and just, belongs to the revolutionary phase of liberation and insurgency. Yet, only the most "fortunate" and politically successful revolutions, such as the American Revolution, Arendt argues, are able to overcome this insurgent phase, channeling their energies into the opening of that space of appearance in which a plurality of equals, leaving behind them the laborious process of liberation, at last experience freedom.

This prompts us to repeat once again, using a terminology extraneous to Arendt's texts but not to their critical spirit, that the experience of insurgent democracy, while often closely intertwined, differs from the completely nonviolent yet thrilling experience of surging democracy. Just as the pathos of those swept up in the collective dynamic of struggle differs from the specific emotion that Arendt calls "public happiness" and reserves for those who, acting in concert, rediscover politics. As if public happiness were indeed characteristic of the initial phase of surging democracy. As if politics were charged with the task of engendering the emotion of public happiness, instead of accumulating and exploiting all the pathos linked to the struggle for liberation, with its almost inevitable burden of "creative violence." As a matter of fact, the affirmative emotion of public happiness does distinguish itself from the pathos of struggle, a pathos, however, with which it remains always in tension. Even more directly, it not only distinguishes itself from but contrasts all of the resentments and hatred that nourish the various populisms of every era. That is, it opposes that affective pathology of negative egocentrism, which, as Arendt cautions in *The Origins of Totalitarianism*, definitively closes every shared space of freedom and ensures that the degeneration of democracy into populist demagoguery becomes a fertile ground for new experiments in "total domination."

3 Public Happiness

IN JANUARY 2018, fifteen hundred students at Yale University enrolled in a course on happiness that turned out to be the most popular, well-attended course in the three hundred years of the prestigious university's existence. Entitled "Psychology and the Good Life," the course aimed to teach students how to live a happier and more satisfying life. The news appeared in the *New York Times*, and from there it spread to the most important newspapers internationally. It was not, however, an absolute novelty. For several years now the University of California, Berkeley, has offered an extremely successful online course on the "Science of Happiness" with other universities following in its wake. The research on happiness has today undoubtedly gained a wide audience. One need only, for that matter, enter any bookstore and take a look at the impressive number of self-help books and booklets, which promise readers the ability to lead a happy life, in order to realize how happiness is currently a topic of prevailing, if not obsessive, interest. There is a full-blown marketing of happiness, directed at individuals, or rather, at their individual, if not intimate, desire for a more satisfying life. Arendt would locate this phenomenon in the sphere of concerns of the private realm, noting that public happiness, as she intends it, is instead what one does not discuss today.

In *The Human Condition*, we read that the word *private*, derived from the Latin *privatus*, alludes to a negative state of deprivation in relation to the light of the public realm. Such a negativity is even more evident in the Greek *idion*, which corresponds to the Latin *privatus*, because for the Greeks, as Arendt writes, "a life spent in the privacy of 'one's own' (*idion*), outside the world of the common, is 'idiotic' by definition."[1] The Arendtian strategy of appealing to etymology in order to diminish the value of the private realm while elevating that of the public one is obvious here. However, what she is principally concerned with, in this context, is not so much this devaluation as the bringing into precise focus of the "ancient borderline between private and political," a fundamental distinction that, according to her, the emergence of modern society has confused and changed, to the point of making unrecognizable "the meaning of the two terms and their significance for the life of the individual and the citizen."[2] This came about, Arendt argues, through a hybridization of the private and the social that, on one hand, produced the ambiguous and omnipresent concept of privacy that torments not only questions of law and, on the other hand, made of the social itself a collective dimension, in which the behavior of the masses replaced the action of plurality. Which, in Arendtian terms, means that the more or less conformist spaces of the private and the social opened up and spread, while the participatory space of politics was systematically eliminated. Or rather, it means that mass society, although it foments and economically exploits the individual desire for a happy life, offers individuals very few opportunities to experience the particular type of political emotion that Arendt calls public happiness.

Arendt elaborates the concept of public happiness in *On Revolution* and in several other works from the early 1960s. Her thesis is that the rediscovery of political freedom during the period of major revolutions resulted, especially for the protagonists of the American Revolution, in the discovery of public happiness. This happiness, like the freedom from which it arose, did not at all refer to "an inner realm into which men might escape at will from the pressure of the world"; on the contrary, it existed and could exist only in that "man-made public space or market-place which antiquity had known as the area where freedom appears and becomes visible to all."[3] This political experience of freedom, "when they had come to taste it," the American revolutionaries called public happiness, "and it consisted in the citizen's right of access to the public realm, in his share in public power . . . as distinct from the generally recognized rights of subjects to be protected by the government in the pursuit of private happiness."[4] Proof of this, Arendt argues, is that for the revolutionary mentality, tyranny was a form of government in which the sovereign monopolized for himself the right of action, thus banishing citizens from public life and confining them to the privacy of their homes and private affairs. "Tyranny, in other words, deprived of public happiness, though not necessarily of private well-being"; that is, it deprived citizens of the experience of participation and of the right to be seen in action, the emotion of acting in concert in a shared space.[5]

Arendt recounts an anecdote on this subject. She notes that the importance of the experience of public happiness for the protagonists of the American Revolution "may be found in the curious hope Jefferson voiced at the end of his life, when he and Adams had begun to discuss, half-jokingly and half-in-earnest, the possibilities of an afterlife." Jefferson's true notion of happiness comes out very clearly, she writes, "when he lets himself go in a mood of playful and sovereign irony and concludes one of his letters to Adams as follow: 'May we meet there again, in Congress, with our ancient Colleagues, and receive with them the seal of approbation: Well done, good and faithful servants.'" In Arendt's view, here, behind the irony, "we have the candid admission that life in Congress, the joy of discourse, . . . of persuading and being persuaded, were to Jefferson not less conclusive a foretaste of an eternal bliss to come than the delight of contemplation had been for medieval piety." Arendt makes it clear that "'the seal of approbation' is not at all the common reward for virtue in a future state; it is the applause, the demonstration of acclaim, 'the esteem of the world,'"[6] corresponding to that "passion for distinction" and "to excel another," which "John Adams held to be 'more essential and remarkable' than any other human faculty."[7]

This clarification on Arendt's part is interesting for several reasons. First of all, because it confirms her belief that the space of the political is essentially a space of mutual visibility where, showing *who* one is through words and deeds, actors exhibit their uniqueness, that is, they fulfill that desire to distinguish themselves, "which makes men love the world and enjoy the company of their peers, and drives them into public business."[8] Second, because it allows Arendt to emphasize that the members of Congress, just like "the people who went to the town assembly," acted "neither exclusively because of

3: Public Happiness

their duty nor, even less, to serve their own interests but most of all because they enjoyed the discussion, the deliberations, and the making of decisions."[9] Pleasure, joy, and even enjoyment: these are the characteristics of public happiness that Arendt mentions here and elsewhere. As if public happiness were the name that synthesizes the positive emotions of those participating in the nascent stage of what we persist in calling surging democracy.

As already in *The Human Condition*, in *On Revolution* the rediscovery of politics by the American revolutionaries again refers to the foundational experience of the Greek *agorà*. It is, however, an innovative rediscovery, capable of creating its own "spontaneous tradition" that, like an increase of wealth peculiar to the "hidden treasure," is passed on from the revolutionary spirit of the eighteenth century to subsequent epochs. Arendt identifies its traces in different and important political phenomena of the twentieth century, from the Workers' Councils of the Hungarian Revolution to the events of the Prague Spring, and she adds to the list the student movement of the 1960s as well. A professor in American universities at the time, Arendt has been able to observe the movement directly and enter into dialogue with it.

Elisabeth Young-Bruehl, an excellent biographer of Arendt, tells us that at the University of Berkeley, in the early days of the movement, one of the texts that circulated most frequently among students was precisely *On Revolution*, and that the newspaper *Public Life*, founded by a group active in Brooklyn, explicitly acknowledged its debt "to two American political theorists: Thomas Jefferson and Hannah Arendt."[10] The movement's interest in Arendt was, in many ways, reciprocated by her. Indeed, as it has been rightly noted, "the student protests gave Arendt the opportunity to write some of her most brilliant essays, in which she tests out categories developed over twenty years of intellectual labor and puts forth new and illuminating distinctions, such as that between power and violence."[11] In one of these essays—a transcription of an interview from 1970—in response to the interviewer's question regarding her opinion of the revolutionary movement of students in western countries, Arendt responds:

> If I consider what (apart from goals, opinions, doctrines) really distinguishes this generation in all countries from earlier generations, then the first thing

that strikes me is its determinations to act, its joy in action, the assurance of being able to change things by one's own effort.... Another experience new for our time entered the game of politics: It turned out that acting is fun. This generation discovered what the eighteenth century had called "public happiness," which means that when man takes part in public life he opens up for himself a dimension of human experience that otherwise remains closed to him and that in some way constitutes a part of complete "happiness."[12]

It should be noted the use of the words *joy* and *fun* as variants of the emotion of public happiness. Even more, we should note the distance that she takes from the goals, opinions, and doctrines of the student movement, which, shortly thereafter, Arendt does not hesitate to denounce for its "theoretical sterility and analytical dullness."[13] Once again, her accent is exclusively on shared action as the rediscovery of public happiness, that is, on interaction as the genuine mode of political experience, regardless of the motivations and contents of the student protest, which Arendt strongly condemns, but which do not affect her positive, if not enthusiastic, judgment of the political nature of the phenomenon. What is striking to her, in other words, is the joyous generational rediscovery of the experience of a surging democracy characterized by a shared, diffuse, and horizontal power, or rather, the rediscovery of the "hidden treasure." What she is interested in is the emphasis on the distinction between this power—or, if one prefers, the revolutionary spirit of the eighteenth century reincarnated in it—and all forms of legitimization of violence. While appreciating the novelty of the nonviolent "participatory democracy" rediscovered by the students, Arendt does not hesitate, in fact, to denounce "the new undeniable glorification of violence by the student movement," the fruit of an "odd loyalty to the past," which is expressed through the old rhetoric of life as struggle and "creative violence."[14] Arendt brusquely observes that "to see the productivity of society in the image of life's 'creativity' is at least as old as Marx, . . . and to think of creativity as man's highest good is at least as old as Bergson."[15] Although students had joyously rediscovered public happiness, their ideology did not resist the most antipolitical siren call of the modern revolutionary myth, that of creative violence.

3: Public Happiness

In the preface to his book on Arendt's political thought,[16] Michael Gottsegen provides useful reflections for understanding the hermeneutical efficacy and empirical plausibility of the Arendtian concept of public happiness. Gottsegen details the words of a conversation with a young Czechoslovakian, who recounted a thrilling experience during the days of the "Velvet Revolution" in Prague in 1989, in which he participated. The young man "spoke of the creation of public spaces where none had existed previously; he spoke of the joy that came with the opportunity to participate in common deliberations with his peers; and he spoke of how his sense of self had changed and deepened with each passing day of engagement in a struggle for what truly mattered." By justly noticing that the story the Czech friend told could have been culled from the last chapter of Hannah Arendt's *On Revolution*, Gottsegen concludes that, although the man had never read Arendt, "he described his experience in the very idiom she used to describe the experience of public happiness." Such a conclusion is completely plausible and, consistent with Arendt's thought, it corroborates her thesis that the phenomenon of public happiness, far from regarding the revolutions of the eighteenth century exclusively, is inherent to the very experience of acting in concert or, at least, to the type of experience our modern political lexicon tends to index under the rubric of "revolution." At stake here, however, is not the concept of revolution itself and even less the "creative violence" that would characterize revolutionary myth, but rather the germinative modality of a political experience characterized by collective enactment and enjoyment of public happiness. Which means, in Arendtian terms, that public happiness, as a specific political emotion, can take place and be recognized, named, and described wherever a plurality acts in concert sharing the joy of manifesting a human condition that is unique and plural. The words of the young man from Prague are not, for that matter, an isolated case. In the vocabulary of those who have the chance to participate in political movements capable of experiencing a surging democracy, terms like *joy* and *happiness* appear quite often in fact. As an example, we only need look at an interesting book of Lynne Segal, dedicated to the feminist movement, emblematically entitled *Radical Happiness: Moments of Collective Joy*. The author focuses in particular on experiences of resistance and renewal, affirmative fulfillment, transformative energy, and shared joy that characterized feminist political performances of the 1960s. Radical happiness, according to her words, evokes, first and foremost, "the significance of a politics of hope" and wells up from the "revival of the revolutionary imagination."[17] While from a very different context, we are indeed not far from the young Czechoslovakian's story of his experience in Prague. The emotion is similar and, regardless of the contents and motivations specific to each scenario, the vocabularies resemble each other.

There is a consonance in the narratives of those who describe the experience of this emotion that wells up from interaction in a public space. There is a common language that accounts for the pathos, individual and collective, inherent to participation. As if surging democracy, on the emotional level, had its own specific lexicon. As if to thrill people in terms of shared joy and happiness were indeed the experience of participation, and consequently the plural "rediscovery" of the political, rather than the movement of struggle and rebellion. Reflecting on Arendt's metaphors, Olivia Guaraldo has rightly noted that where Arendt insists on the "rediscovery" of the "lost treasure" of participatory politics, she suggests that such a rediscovery refers to something familiar: something not yet known and that, however, is immediately recognizable. This "can be confirmed by the fact that political actors, almost always, recognize it as something very familiar when they act."[18] Which means that the "treasure" of acting in concert, although "hidden" by a tradition that for centuries concealed and buried it in the past, is, however, very close, almost within reach, for those who "rediscover" it in the present. Public happiness, "forgotten by theory and codified language, yet very familiar to political experience,"[19] more than taking actors by surprise, surprises them precisely because of its taste of familiarity, almost like an emotion forgotten but known and recognized. Almost as if that which Arendt calls "the taste of public freedom" had precisely its own recognizable flavor.

In a text written after *On Revolution* and recently published by Jerome Khon under the very meaningful title of "The Freedom to Be Free," Arendt connects, in a quite explicit and particularly rich way, the theme of revolution to the category of natality. Arendt writes that for the actors of the American Revolution, the experience of being free coincided, or rather was intimately interwoven, with beginning something new, with, metaphorically speaking, the birth of a new era. To be free and to start something new were felt to be the same. And obviously, this mysterious human gift, the ability to start something new, has something to do with the fact that every one of us came into the world as a newcomer through birth. In other words, we can begin something because we *are* beginnings and hence beginners. [Because] birth or human natality is the ontological condition *sine qua non* of all politics . . . the meaning of revolution is the actualization of one of the greatest and most elementary human potentialities, the unequaled experience of *being* free to make a new beginning, from which comes the pride of having opened the world to a *Novus Ordo Saeclorum*.[20]

The experience of public happiness, for Arendt, has to do precisely with this beginner's pride, which, in order to find expression, requires a shared space of appearance. It is by appearing to others that political actors joyously actualize their ontological condition, rooted in birth, of being unique and beginners. There is something surging, indeed nascent and beginning, in the manifestation of public happiness: as if public happiness were the name of the collective, and at the same time individual, emotion that wells up from the experience of participation and of being in relation with others. Taking several lines of Jefferson and Adams, in this regard, Arendt speaks of "passion for distinction" and "desire to excel another." Far from betraying an exhibitionist vein, this type of vocabulary, already present in *The Human Condition*, takes its inspiration from the Aristotelian concept of virtue as excellence, *areté*, a concept that Arendt explicitly appreciates. In *On Revolution*, her accent falls expressly on the relational dimension of plurality as a theater and also a stimulus for excellence. Put another way, the presence of others is necessary so that the passion for distinction and the desire to excel another can be realized; that is, it is necessary so that participants actively share in the experience of public happiness and recognize its taste.

Public happiness literally has need of a public, of a common space in which those present mutually appear as actors and spectators, interacting on a horizontal plane. As the word suggests, *happiness* is something that *happens* when, by interacting, we actively disclose the unique distinction and capacity for initiative that make us human. "Events, by definition, are occurrence that interrupt routine process and routine procedures," notes Arendt.[21] The experience of public happiness occurs, happens, springs up when we reactivate, in public, the ontological traits of our having been born unique and beginners.

The interesting link between the noun "happiness" and the verb "to happen" finds etymological confirmation, in English, in terms like *perhaps* and *haphazard*, which evoke the concept of chance, fortune, or luck. The same can be said for the German *Glück* and the French *bonheur*. The etymon is different for the Italian *felicità*, which—like the Spanish *felicidad*, the Portuguese *felicitade*, the English *felicity*, and the French *félicité*—obviously derives from the Latin *felix*, to whose root can also be attributed terms like fecundity, fertility, feminine, and fetus. The root is the same for the Greek verb *phyo*, meaning "to generate" or "to give birth," and for the noun *physis*, meaning "nature," a noun that is in turn, and not by chance, related to the Latin verb *nasci* ("to be born"). It seems, therefore, that in various languages, the concept of happiness is split between two seemingly opposed registers of meaning: one that alludes to luck or fortune, the other that alludes instead to the feminine sphere of fertility and birth.

Indeed, there is something happy—or, better, felicitous—in birth or, as Arendt would say, something that is linked to the newborn who makes her entry into the world, appears there, and exhibits herself to others as unique and beginner. Here it is worth again quoting the passage from *The Human Condition* in which Arendt affirms that, with action, "we insert ourselves into the human world, and this insertion is like a second birth, in which we confirm and take upon ourselves the naked fact of our original physical appearence."[22] And it is worth repeating that, in Arendtian terms, natality functions as the ontological condition of political action and thus of public happiness. Making use of the etymologies described above, we could therefore say that natality as felicity is the premise and the basis for public happiness. In English, the etymological wordplay does not work perfectly well, actually. The noun happiness evokes chance or fortune, not birth. Which means that the Italian *felicità* and all of the languages that express the concept conserved in the Latin *felix* have the surprising virtue of etymologically accentuating the nascent and germinal quality of public happiness that Arendt praises.

Popular wisdom famously celebrates birth as "a happy event." Birth engenders happiness or, better yet, felicity. At stake, however, is not simply a private felicity, the family's felicity, but rather, as Arendt would say, a felicity that concerns the whole world, enriched by the new entry of a unique human being whose characteristic is that of beginning new things and therefore changing the world itself through action. In short, action inherits and reactivates the felicity of birth. Public happiness, in Arendtian terms, is part of this process, that is, it brings to fulfillment, not only practically, but also emotionally, the initial promise.

Ancient Greek has basically two words for designating happiness: *eudaimonia* and *makaria*. Although they are often used as synonyms, *makarios* tends to refer to the privileged status of the gods who, according to Aristotle, are perfectly happy because their life consists of ceaseless contemplation.[23] It is worth noting that, in Latin, *makarios* is usually rendered as *beatus*, as is apparent, among other things, in the text of the Sermon on the Mount (Matthew 5:3–11), in which we find a series of those who are blessed (*beati*), corresponding, in the Greek version, to *makarioi*.

As for the term *eudaimonia*, used most commonly to indicate human happiness, this is composed of two parts: *eu*, meaning "good," and *daimon*, a term generally translated as "daemon," but whose multilayered meaning is difficult to define. Examining the old proverb that says "call no man happy (*eudaimon*) until he is dead," Arendt suggests that the word *eudaimonia* "means literally something like the well-being of the *daimon* who accompanies each man throughout life, who is his distinct identity, but appears and is visible only to others," that is, "a lasting state of being which is neither subject to change nor capable of effecting change."[24] It is important to again notice her accent on the expository and relational character of identity as embodied uniqueness, as a revelation of *who* one is. According to Arendt, the Greek notion of *daimon* indicates the unique identity of each human being, that is, the very uniqueness that human beings reveal to one another when, interacting in a shared space of appearance, they publicly disclose *who* they are.

To be *eudaimon*, Arendt notes, is for Aristotle the same thing as "living well" (*eu zen*).[25] This note is interesting because, in Aristotelian terms, *eudaimon* applies both to "living well" (*eu zen*) and "doing well" (*eu prattein*), that is, leading an excellent life fulfilling what is proper of man as *zoon logon echon* and *zoon politikon*. In fact, we read, in a famous passage of Aristotle's *Politics*, that man alone of the animals possesses speech and is a political animal by nature;[26] or, to borrow Arendt's much more incisive translation, that man is "a being attaining his highest possibility in the faculty of speech and the life in a polis."[27] In another famous passage of *Politics*, Aristotle affirms that the polis, although generated as a means to secure life (*zen*), exists for the purpose of good life (*eu zen*).[28] Merely living *in* the polis, cohabitating, living together, is thus clearly distinguished by Aristotle from actively living the experience *of* the polis, and subordinated to this. Pushing Arendt's filter to the extremes, one could even argue that Aristotle already indicates in the *agorà* a space of public happiness. As it is useful to point out, there are, however, few people who enjoy this public happiness, that is, to only speak of Athens, only free, male citizens, born of Athenian parents, while the majority of the population—composed of women, slaves, and the other inhabitants of the city—are notoriously excluded from it. Consequently, felicity in terms of fecundity—if we wish to insist upon the etymon explored above—is structurally excluded from the political sphere of happiness that Aristotle calls on: whether or not definable as public happiness, the *eu zen* corresponding to the good life in the polis, according to Aristotle, concerns only human beings in the fullest sense, intended by him as free, male citizens. They are, not by chance, the same human beings that, when absorbed in philosophical contemplation, can even be happy (*makarioi*) like the gods. In conclusion, we must therefore confront the fact that the original Greek experience of politics, the model of the *agorà* that would be the basis for the idea of democracy, is characterized by a weighty patriarchal and slave-owning stigma. A fact that Arendt duly notes but that, according to many of her interpreters, she does not satisfactorily problematize, or treats in a decidedly disturbing way.[29] Applying an Arendtian lens to reread Aristotle remains, however, an endeavor that can bear interesting fruit. This is evidenced by an Arendtian scholar like John Kiess, who underlines how, for Aristotle, the *eu zen*, living well, "is not a state achieved when action is complete, but a state of activity"; likewise, "action is not a means to *eudaimonia*, but constitutive of *eudaimonia*," so that virtues (*aretai*), as the expression and realization of human excellence, "are not simply tools that help us eventually arrive at happiness, but are themselves a tangible taste of happiness."[30] Referring to the Greek world and to the polis as a theater for accomplishing great and memorable deeds, Arendt, in fact, argues that such a "greatness, or the specific meaning of each deed, can lie only in the performance itself and neither in its motivation nor its achievement."[31] Exemplary, in this sense, is for her the notion of *energeia*, with which Aristotle "designated all activities that do not pursue an end and leave no work behind, but exhaust their full meaning in the performance itself"; likewise, Arendt notes, we could say of *eu zen*: it is not a work, a product of the polis in terms of an organization of life or living together, "but exists only in sheer actuality."[32] As in the case of flute playing, the meaning of the act is entirely in the execution and, in Arendtian terms, there is happiness in this act, just as there is happiness in "the highest and greatest activities of man," which pertain to the realm of politics and action.

To act politically produces a type of happiness different and higher than any private activity, Arendt affirms. Contrary to the perfect happiness of contemplation, divine but solitary, this happiness entails a being-in-relation. It is the human condition of plurality itself that actively manifests itself in this emotion of relational and beginner subjectivities. One understands, therefore, why Arendt defines freedom in terms of spontaneity. Public happiness is not something that is planned and calculated, but rather precisely "happens" when human beings act in concert in a shared space of appearance. In other words, by surprising them with its familiar character, public happiness is discovered and rediscovered by political actors whenever and wherever they perform for the sake of the "freedom to be free," thus tasting the constitutive, birthing quality of action.

During the same years that Adams and Jefferson were experiencing public happiness in America, Jeremy Bentham was reformulating, in England, the famous axiom of the "greatest happiness of the greatest number," in the belief that it was the duty of governments to promote the well-being of society.[33] The formula has enjoyed considerable success, not only within the various theoretical currents of utilitarianism, but also within the universe of political, sociological, and liberal studies, just as varied, which conceive of happiness in terms of that social well-being of citizens that governments are called on to ensure and promote, if not to produce. With a certain prophetic concern, Alexis de Tocqueville, an author beloved by Arendt, goes so far as to imagine, in his reflections on *Democracy in America* (1840), "an immense tutelary power, which alone takes charge of assuring subjects' enjoyments and watching over their fate," a power "absolute, detailed, regular, far-seeing, and mild," which "works for their happiness," keeps them "fixed irrevocably in childhood . . . foresees and secures their needs, facilitates their pleasures."[34] The idea of this form of pervasive and infantilizing government, which Tocqueville does not hesitate to define as "administrative despotism," is obviously extreme. But the concern that inspires it touches on a problem that, over time, has turned into a model of governmentality in which the method, evaluation, and detail indeed play a decisive role. Essentially, today the image of a society constructed on the principle of happiness-maximization is that of a society whose level of well-being is measurable on the basis of various economic indices, objective and subjective, to which are added factors like health, education, quality of services, lifestyle, and safety.[35] Publicizing scholarly research that work on these indices, newspapers today often offer charts that rank the nation's "happiest cities," or rather, the cities in which there is the best quality of life. In Italy, on average Trento and Bolzano occupy the top positions. In the classification of European nations, Finland has finished first for several years now.

Of a different type, but nevertheless very topical, is the kind of approach that instead views individual and social happiness in terms of desire for and enjoyment of consumerism. We are here, to use Tocqueville's description, in the sphere of the "facilitation of pleasures." Or, to use Arendt's words, in the sphere in which reigns "the greedier and more craving appetites" and in which "no object of the world will be safe from consumption and annihilation through consumption."[36] Critical studies on consumer society, and on the economic strategy that nourishes it, speak, in this sense, of compulsive desire, inexhaustible pleasure, frenzy, and hedonistic neuroses. The subject, of course, is too complex to be addressed in a few words here, but it offers a valuable cue for avoiding confusing the Arendtian concept of public happiness and the sociological, psychological, political, and, especially, economic and liberal notion of happiness—collective or private, utilitarian or hedonistic— which contemporary debates focus on. The bibliography on the subject is, indeed, impressive, passing easily from specialized studies to general belief. Remaining on a general level, one need only recall that the United Nations has, since 2013, organized the yearly celebration of World Happiness Day, and that each year it publishes an *Annual Happiness Report*, whose indices serve as reference for other similar classifications. In addition, an academic journal exists, entitled *Journal of Happiness*, which covers an extremely vast and varied thematic repertory. Impressive, as mentioned above, is the number of multidisciplinary publications that, revisiting Bentham's principle of the maximization of happiness, analyze, with evidence and tables, how and to what extent government technologies today are adept at measuring, adjusting, producing, and assuring a certain standard of individual and social happiness. The topic of public happiness as a quintessential political emotion receives, in contrast, little attention.[37] As for happiness as the insatiable pleasure of consumerism, and therefore as the entertainment and satisfaction of any hedonist impulse: this serves as a perfect counterbalance to a lack of attention to public happiness, which is conceivably one of the reasons for the success of the university courses and self-help books on happiness mentioned above, which promise students and readers the chance to escape the neurosis consumer society generates by means of a sort of internal beatitude.

The anomaly of Arendt within the history of political thought therefore stands out clearly from this point of observation, too; which makes the Arendtian concept of public happiness seemingly outdated but, at the same time, extraordinarily topical, if, by embracing Arendt's perspective, we begin to observe several political phenomena of the present through different eyes. It depends on the opportunities we have to experience the emotions of these phenomena and on our ability to find the words to express them. Such opportunities, to speak only of recent times, have occurred frequently. For example, with the Women's March, in January 2017, when millions of women flooded the squares of Washington, D.C., and of hundreds of other cities around the world, participating in demonstrations of resistance and protest described as experiences of affirmative energy and joy. Or, for example, with the March for Our Lives, in March 2018 in Florida and elsewhere, when thousands of young people, some very young, were able to share the experience of exercising in a shared space, as had students in 1968, their right to free speech as a basic component of public happiness. And, last but not least, with the vast Global Climate Strike, on March 15, 2019, which saw children and teenagers protesting peacefully and joyfully, suddenly discovering the emotion of participative politics.

There is, obviously, a quantitative leap—that we must eventually problematize—in this type of approach, which applies the Arendtian category of plurality to a larger collective subjectivity. Just as there is an obvious effort to accentuate the emotion of participation at the expense of that of protest. Yet, if we have in mind certain pages of Arendt's *On Revolution*, the impression of a genuine rediscovery of public happiness, even in the present day and age, remains. Almost as if these forms of marches and demonstrations, although indeed fed by a movement of resistance and protest, and although characterized by a number of participants that dilates the political space to the extreme and thus threatens the very plausibility of the concept of plurality, were the modern-day forms of an experience of the political in which actors "happen" to experience the emotion of a surging democracy. That is to say, almost as if they were spaces of participation in which participants "happen" to discover and recognize that public happiness is transmitted from generation to generation like a hidden treasure.

4
Political Squares

IN HIS AUTOBIOGRAPHICAL NOVEL *The Return: Fathers, Sons and the Land in Between*, Libyan writer Hisham Matar, who for several years has been living and working in London, recounts his return to Libya in 2012 in search of the truth regarding the fate of his father, an opponent of the Gaddafi regime who, in 1990, was arrested and definitively "disappeared" in Libyan jails.[1] Matar meets friends and relatives, including his cousin Marwan, a judge from Benghazi who describes his own personal involvement in the start of the Arab Spring in Libya. Marwan recounts how, on the night of February 15, 2011, two days before the revolution began, together with a dozen colleagues, he had organized a protest against the arrest of Fathi Terbil, a lawyer who had represented the families of more than a thousand political prisoners killed in the prisons of the dictator. Performing an act that they themselves considered "nothing more than a symbolic gesture," they stood on the steps of the Benghazi courthouse "in the cold winter breeze, with the sea, invisible in the night, murmuring in the background." The following evening, they were again at their posts before the courthouse, fearing a crackdown. "Instead, what emerged through the surrounding dark streets were the families of the deceased . . . hundreds of people came, and the following day the number grew into the thousands. On the 17th of February, the date after which the revolution was named, the authorities attacked and killed several demonstrators. Instead of scaring people away, it had the

45

opposite effect." The crowd grew and people continued to come together and to demonstrate. No longer emerging from darkness like on the night of protest on the courthouse steps, bodies now showed themselves in full light, conspicuous and resistant. Matar tells us that a new newspaper was founded at that time, entitled *Al-Mayadin*, which means "squares." The editors had wanted to call it that because "the revolutions in Tunisia, Egypt and here all broke out from public squares."[2]

Clearly, the journalists at *Al-Mayadin* understood that the political peculiarity of the phenomenon lay precisely in what was taking place in the squares: squares crowded, day and night, with thousands of people proclaiming their right, not only to be there and to speak out, but to live and survive, sleep and eat, in a public space. Even western observers, who coined the expression Arab Spring, understood that this was a unique political experience, centered on the role and functional organization of the city square. Indeed, if it is true that squares invaded by the crowd belong to the traditional revolutionary imaginary, these Arab squares nevertheless appeared different, organized to last as public spaces of resistance and coexistence: with tent cities equipped with distribution points for food and water, first-aid posts, and facilities for the administration of medical care. As Judith Butler has rightly highlighted in *Notes Toward a Performative Theory of Assembly*, bodies and the bodily needs of life come to the fore, in this case, in the shared space of resistance and protest. Butler refers, moreover, not only to Arab squares but also to political phenomena that reanimated the model of this elsewhere. The squares of the Arab Spring were in fact contagious. Broadcast worldwide via television and internet, their image inspired movements and modes of protest in other squares across the planet. Today "access to any public squares presupposes access to some media that relay the events outside of that space and time."[3] With remarkable rapidity, experiences universally designated as "movement of the squares" and "politics of the street" ended up becoming a widespread phenomenon; characterized, although in a diversity of varying contexts, by a common emphasis on the putting into practice of a democracy rigorously horizontal, direct, inclusive, and without leaders.[4] The Indignados in Spain, whose motto was *Toma la plaza!*—"Take the square!"—called it real democracy and defended its horizontality and heterogeneity even against the inevitable tendency of activists to take initiatives and to speak for everyone.[5]

When Butler published *Notes Toward a Performative Theory of Assembly*, in 2015, the phenomenon of political squares had already spread around the world. The American philosopher cites, among the most well-known scenes, that of Occupy Wall Street in New York, the Indignados in Spain, and Gezi Park in Istanbul, but also refers to a myriad of events, big or small and more or less enduring, that she summarizes under the name of "demonstrating precarity." The focal point of Butler's reflection is the assembly form of a political interaction that finds its place of expression in a public space occupied and enlivened by real bodies. It is precisely this corporeal dimension that is at the center of Butler's attention and that allows her to revisit the concept of democracy in an original way. "When bodies assemble on the street, in the square, or in other forms of public space," writes Butler, we cannot "say 'this is democracy in action,' and mean that everything we expect of democracy is emblematized or enacted by such a moment. Gatherings are necessarily transient, and that transience is linked to their critical function"; which, Butler concludes, means that "gatherings such as these serve as one of democracy's incipient or 'fugitive' moments."[6] One could thus speak, with good reason, of surging democracy, a democracy observed precisely at its incipient moment. Butler's insistence on bodies, on their performative acts, and on their exhibition of the precarity of corporeal life, gives, however, her discourse a particular twist: "it matters when public squares are filled to the brim, when people eat and sleep there, sing and refuse to cede that space, as we saw in the first gathering in Tahrir Square, and continue to see in other parts of the world."[7] According to her, what we see at work, when bodies assemble in public squares or march in the street, is in fact "their right to appear, to exercise freedom," while "demanding a livable life."[8] Butler's thesis is clear:

> Indeed, in the politics of the street that has been with us in the last years, in the Occupy Movement, Tahrir Square in its early stage, Puerta del Sol, Gezi Park, and the favela movement in Brazil, the basic requirements of the body are at the center of political mobilization—*those requirements are, in fact, publicly enacted prior to any set of political demands*. Over and against

forces of privatization, the destruction of public services and the ideals of the public good precipitated by the takeover of neoliberal forms of rationality in governance and everyday life, bodies require food and shelter, protection from injury and violence, and the freedom to move, to work, to have access to health care; bodies require other bodies for support and for survival.[9]

It is a matter, insists Butler, of performative bodies that share "a space of appearance," confirming and displaying their essential condition of plurality and, especially, of precarity.

In this book, more so than in others, Butler's reference to Arendtian vocabulary is intentional and explicit. First of all, Butler appreciates in Arendt the category of plurality and the understanding of politics as space of appearance. Emphasizing several times that "to be a political actor is a function, a feature of acting on terms of equality," Butler acknowledges that "this important Arendtian formulation remains relevant to contemporary democratic struggles."[10] She, however, inexorably distances herself from Arendt and severely critiques her on a crucial issue. The issue, for Butler a fundamental one, concerns the expressivity of bodies in relation to the demands for livable lives, that is, the "bodily dimension of action" becoming all the more apparent "in those cases when political struggle is about food, employment, mobility, and access to institutions."[11]

The principal object of Butler's critique is the Arendtian distinction between the public realm and the private realm, the first intended as the ambit of acting in concert and therefore of politics, the second intended as the ambit in which, through labor, one provides for the reproduction and the care of bodies and thus for the biological necessities of life. This is a point that has been much discussed in the critical literature on Arendt, and, notably, a point on which is based her even more discussed separation of the political sphere from the economic and social one. Referring to the interpretations of "various feminist theorists," Butler observes that the model of the ancient polis, to which Arendt appeals in order to distinguish the public realm from the private one, reserved the former for free males and the latter for women and slaves: a fact, as mentioned above, that Arendt duly registers, but to which she does not devote satisfactory critical arguments. It is not, moreover, so much the issue of gender or the sexism of the ancient polis that annoys Butler, but rather the Arendtian thesis according to which the ambit of labor and of the biological necessities of life is pre-political and nonpolitical, and as such therefore excluded from the public space of appearance. Put another way, although Arendt insists upon the spatial and material dimension of political interaction, that is, on the embodied presence of actors that act in concert, everything that concerns the needs of their bodies—along with the labor that provides for these needs—is pushed by her *outside* of this plural theater and relegated to the private realm, in which, as Butler clarifies, "we find the question of needs, the reproduction of the material conditions of life, and the problems of transience, reproduction, and death alike—everything that pertains to precarious life."[12] To put it concisely, for Arendt, the experience of public freedom requires the presence of bodies, but it does not care for bodies. Writes Butler: "Arendt's view clearly meets its limits here, for the body is itself divided into one that appears publicly to speak and act and another one, sexual, laboring, feminine, foreign, and mute, that generally is relegated to the private and pre-political sphere. Such a division of labor is precisely what is called into question when precarious lives assemble on the street in form of alliance that must struggle to achieve a space of appearance."[13] The life of the body—its hunger, its need of shelter and of protection from violence—becomes a major issue of politics.[14]

The reasons for Butler's dissent in regard to Arendt's thought are summed up efficaciously when the American philosopher declares: "Although Arendt theorizes the problem of the body, the located body, the speaking body emerging into the 'space of appearance' as part of any political action, she is not quite willing to affirm a politics that struggles to overcome inequalities in food distribution, that affirm rights of housing, and that targets inequalities in the sphere of reproductive labor."[15]

In short, Arendt resoundingly expels from politics the so-called social question, however one intends it. Which, in light of the fact that, historically, democracy has been the means by which the poor and dispossessed have tried to access politics in order to change their condition, makes rethinking the very idea of democracy, by appealing to Arendt, extremely complicated. But it makes it even more arduous to rethink democracy in a radical way, as Butler does, by placing at the center of the democratic stage, understood as "space of appearance," precisely the basic needs of bodies and their condition of precarity. As Butler well knows, and duly mentions, the most unpalatable point of the Arendtian hostility toward the inclusion of bodily needs within the realm of politics is expressed in her anomalous and almost scandalous interpretation of the French Revolution.

One of Arendt's central, and most contested, theses in *On Revolution* maintains that the French Revolution, contrary to the American one, was only marginally able to actualize the emotion of public happiness because of the centrality of the social question to its revolutionary scene, embodied by the poor, who, driven by hunger and need, inundated the streets of Paris like "a torrent rushing forward with elemental force," struggling for liberation from "the necessity of biological life itself"; "the result was that necessity invaded the political realm, the only realm where men can be truly free."[16] From that moment on, continues Arendt, "the 'real wants' determined the course of the Revolution,"[17] bequeathing to posterity that concept of revolution as irresistible and violent movement of insurgent crowds, which still stands out in the western political imaginary. In other words, according to Arendt, whereas the American Revolution discovered the experience of public happiness that our revolutionary imaginary was unfortunately not able to inherit and must therefore "rediscover" every time anew, the French Revolution instead allowed the impossible desire of the multitudes for ridding themselves of the necessities of life to wrongfully invade—in both its modes and contents—the political realm of freedom and to prevail in our perception of the revolutionary paradigm. Indeed, as it is worth repeating, in Arendtian terms it is, first and foremost, a matter of bringing into focus the contrast between the movement of *liberation*—not just from oppression, but from hunger and from destitution—and the shared experience of political *freedom*. Therefore, as Butler rightly notes, "the political domain is once again adamantly distinguished from the domain of economic need," with the added clarification that, for Arendt, not only "those who act from necessity act from the body," but "freedom can only be achieved by those who are well, not hungry."[18]

Even in prior writings in which she engages with Arendt, Butler does not hide her repulsion for the Arendtian valorization of a political model such as that of the Greek *polis*, which entails slavery. In *Who Sings the Nation-State?*

Language, Politics, Belonging, Butler notes that in this model there intervenes "a certain political mechanism of deprivation that works first through categorizing those who may or may not exercise freedom."[19] Placed in the domestic sphere of labor and reproduction, women and slaves are deprived of the capacity to be free. Almost as if the very elaboration of the concept of the "public realm" required, for Arendt, an expulsive device for nonpolitical and servile types of life. Certainly, as Butler acknowledges in *Notes Toward a Performative Theory of Assembly*, to think a radical democracy with Arendt means, in these and in other occasions, to think it against Arendt.

The fact remains that Arendt, focusing her attention on the direct, materially participated-in, and nonrepresentative form of politics that emerged in ancient Greece, has the merit of reelaborating it by proposing an idea of politics that exalts the relationality at work within an embodied plurality. Butler is, indeed, more than willing to appropriate these Arendtian categories in order to conceptualize the specific assembly and performative form of politics dear to her, a form characterized by the plural interaction and corporeal exposure of people who occupy and share a public space of appearance.

The first step of this conceptualization, writes Butler, consists in approaching "a notion of plurality that is thought together with both performativity and interdependency,"[20] which, in her lexicon, means a shared precarity and a common preoccupation with enacting, in the same place of appearance, the conditions that make lives livable. What matters most, in fact, in Butler's view of these crowded and politicized squares, is not only the phenomenon of people who gather and demonstrate, but also their reciprocal commitment to engender, in the place they occupy, a new form of sociality in which the needs of bodies—food, shelter, protection from injury and violence—are taken care of. And Arendt certainly cannot support this point, which is vital for Butler, who asserts that "precarity is indissociable from that dimension of politics that addresses the organization and protection of bodily needs."[21]

Butler is right to affirm that the participative democracy imagined by Arendt posits the presence of bodies or, in Butler's terms, of bodies that speak, communicate, signify in a public space of appearance. That is, she is right to emphasize that "for Arendt, political action takes place on the condition that the body appear."[22] The problem still remains that, although Arendt insists upon the physical dimension of the space of appearance—a space opened by a plurality of actor-spectators who want and need to be seen and heard by each other—she, however, not only abstains from focusing her own attention on the body in a convincing manner, but, furthermore, programmatically displaces elsewhere the question of the various concrete needs that the corporeal condition brings with it. Everything that relates to this question remains obscured—private matters that are pre-political and nonpolitical. In opposition to Arendt, Butler instead asserts that bodies that gather in public spaces, exhibiting their precarity and producing "the conditions under which vulnerability and interdependency become livable," draw "critical attention to the condition of bodily survival, persistence, and flourishing within the framework of radical democracy."[23] Above all, Butler insists on the broad spectrum of material signification inherent to the performativity of plural bodies, "the performativity of the human animal [that] takes place through gesture, gait, modes of mobility, sound and image, and various expressive means that are not reducible to public forms of verbal speech."[24] In substance, therefore, and to put it a bit drastically, while Arendt, faithful to the Aristotelian definition of man as *zoon logon echon*, believes that speech is what essentially matters in the "speaking body" that acts in a public space, Butler believes that "the way we gather on the street, sing or chant, or even maintain our silence can be, and is part of, the performative dimension of politics, situating speech as one bodily act among others."[25] The question is crucial, because it broadens the phenomenology of the political to include the vocal dimension, that is, it suggests that these incipient moments of surging democracy possess their own peculiar phonosphere. In regards to speech as verbal activity, Butler indeed pushes her reflection even further, emphasizing the primary role of vocality, that is, of the signification of plural bodies that express their corporeal uniqueness by making themselves heard vocally. This is, moreover, coherent with her general thesis that "forms of assembly already signify prior to, and apart from, any particular demands they make," given that their embodied and plural performativity "signifies in excess of whatever is said."[26] Vocalization requires a larynx, notes Butler; the plurality of bodies

4: Political Squares

needs organs of vocalization to express itself, not only to speak but also to produce sounds that signify politically, exceeding the sphere of speech. Almost as if public happiness, as Arendt would call it, indeed had its own specific plural voice, a peculiar sonority, a unique political phonosphere.

Butler, to tell the truth, does not speak of happiness in *Notes Toward a Performative Theory of Assembly*, and, contrary to Arendt, does not take into consideration the eventuality that happiness is a political category. Yet, if observed with Arendtian eyes, Butler's enthusiasm for the assembly phenomenology and its innovative political valence seems precisely to allude to the felicitous moment of a nascent and germinal form of democracy. That this form is transitory and often does not result in suitable outcomes—but rather, on the contrary, in depressing and profoundly alarming ones—is well known. In Libya, the phenomenon of the Arab Spring certainly did not give the hoped-for outcome for those who had mobilized for democracy. In this regard, Butler lucidly observes that, among the political squares seen in the past few years, many "have produced new state formations or conditions of war that are surely as problematic as those they replaced."[27] Symptomatically, referring back once more to the ancient world, Arendt underlines that, for the Greeks, "the innermost meaning of the acted deed and the spoken word is independent of victory and defeat and must remain untouched by any eventual outcome, by their consequences for better or worse."[28] And, reminding us that action resembles a "miracle,"[29] she warns us, moreover, that the opening of political spaces of appearance through interaction, including revolutionary interaction, is a rare and intermittent phenomenon in human history. History, in fact, often presents us with the occurrence of new systems of power that supplant or violently close the felicitous experiences of the public realm, or even transform such experiences into despotic forms of domination. In a certain sense, at least to the extent that Butler focuses on the phenomenology of contemporary political squares in their temporal transience and does not fail to point out their often disappointing outcomes, she is therefore genuinely Arendtian. And she is so on other decisive points as well. It is indeed not by chance that Butler's notion of radical democracy, not unlike the Arendtian notion of power, programmatically expels violence from the political sphere of appearance. What, in fact, appears here are above all bodies that have encountered violence, but who want neither to return nor to reanimate it. Butler strongly emphasizes that "assemblies of this kind can succeed only if they subscribe to principles of nonviolence," that is, only if they confront violence "without reproducing its terms," showing in this way "how the nonviolent resistance to violence is possible."[30]

Butler's interest in Arendt—which in *Notes Toward a Performative Theory of Assembly* focuses especially on a valorization of the concepts of plurality and space of appearance—manifests itself already in previous texts, in which the American philosopher, revisiting the topic of stateless persons and refugees, takes up with conviction the Arendtian critique of the nation-state. Butler appreciates, in Arendt, the view of a plurality that is not only interactive, but inclusive and nonviolent. Put another way, although Butler often distances herself from Arendt, in her reading of Arendt's texts it is possible to trace out a tenacious constructive thread that exalts, from the beginning, the promising union between politics and nonviolence. Butler, first and foremost, looks for and finds in Arendt a style of thinking that, in addition to courageously confronting contemporary events, knows how to conjugate a critique of violence with the imagination of a political form that, more than simply opposing or reacting to oppressive political systems, presents the innovative features of a model aimed at exalting the freedom and the spontaneity of plural interaction. In this respect, the relationship of Butler to the most original categories of Arendt's work is productive and sound. The same cannot be said of the topic of precarity of intensely vulnerable lives and of that series of problems, ever more urgent in the globalized world, which we could summarize under the rubric of poverty and social justice. Coming to terms with Arendt means coming to terms with this limit, that is, coming to terms with a position that radically postulates an autonomy of the political. It means registering that what Arendt provides, first and foremost, for our reflection is the pure concept of a political reality that corresponds to the phenomenology of a democracy observed in its phase of springing-up and in its contingent and fragile becoming. Motivations, contents, and outcomes are indeed outside this framework.

4: Political Squares

"Power springs up between men when they act together and vanishes the moment they disperse," writes Arendt, and it is "to an astonishing degree independent of material factors, either of numbers or means."[31] In other words, the Arendtian plurality is a *qualitative* plurality, rather than a *quantitative* one—the number of those present is not what counts; what counts is the political quality of their acting in concert.[32] Precisely the spatial dimension inherent to this acting ends up, however, with imposing material limits, suggesting that the number of actors cannot exceed a certain quantity. In order to interact in a shared space, Arendt often repeats, those present must see and hear each other; the ideal dimension is the *agorà*: a square, a hall, a place sufficiently large to contain everyone.

One can then question whether, following Butler in applying the Arendtian category of "space of appearance" to the "political squares" of our time and, especially, to the streets crowded by "bodies who are demonstrating," we have not forced the issue too strongly. That Arendt would have defined as genuinely political the phenomenon of assembled bodies that march in protest is, moreover, unlikely. By forcing the Arendtian space of appearance to include this type of demonstration, with the help of Butler's texts, we have ventured into a philologically incorrect operation.

In truth, it is a very useful operation, which finally confronts us with an important and now inescapable issue. It compels us, in fact, to thematize, without further deferrals, the tension, not devoid of disturbing points of confusion and permeability, that connects the scene in which the crowd moves and the scene in which plurality stands out. With a third and highly crucial inconvenience, well known in the political thought of the nineteenth century, that sooner or later one must name: the scene of the masses. Here at stake are three scenes, not only different but on which hangs an immense critical literature. Put another way, the terms *plurality* and *masses*, between which that apparently more nuanced term *crowd* at times acts as a bridge, occupy quite different and, to be precise, opposed, positions in the organizational chart of the political lexicon and the phenomenology of collective subjects we are grappling with. And it is precisely the Arendtian category of plurality, that we have adopted with a certain enthusiasm, that compels us to account for the implications of this type of lexicon and for the problems of this phenomenology. As Butler well knows, the assemblies of bodies do not always express the public happiness of a qualitatively plural, surgent democracy. Nor do the collective subjects that occupy the squares and march in the streets always do so for the sake, even emotional, of an incipient democracy. The issue is crucial and not at all simple. Which criteria allow us to distinguish the plurality from the crowd and, above all, from the masses?

DUO

Political Phonospheres

5

The Voice of the Masses

THERE IS A CRUCIAL PROBLEM whispered among the most cautious Arendtians when they think that no one is listening to them. It is the same problem that every attempt to rethink democracy today in its surging state must sooner or later come to terms with. Judith Butler formulates it explicitly when she writes: "I am certainly not saying that all bodies collected in the street are a good thing or that we should celebrate mass demonstrations, or that bodies assembled form a certain idea of community or even a new politics worthy of praise."[1] The assembly of bodies and the squares packed with bodies are not intrinsically positive or negative, "they assume differing values depending on what they are assembled for, and how that assembly works."[2] The phenomenon of people gathering "can refer equally well to right-wing demonstrations, to military soldiers assembled to quell demonstrations or seize power, to lynch mobs or anti-immigrant populist movements taking over public space."[3] And, we could add, in order to ideologically balance the view, it can also refer to demonstrations, as in the cases of the Black Bloc or the Yellow Vest protest movements, whose mobilization flows into acts of vandalism, destruction, and violence. In short, we need a criterion for defining as "democratic" a political square, and, even more so, a crowd of demonstrators on the march. For Butler, the criterion consists of declaring desirable only forms of assembly working "in the service of realizing greater ideals of justice and equality, even the realization of democracy itself."[4] It is not

59

enough to look to the material phenomenology of the square, to that which Butler often designates as "assembly of bodies," in order to speak of democracy. What also counts, and even prior, are the motivations, the values, the contents, the ideas that this assembly expresses, as well as the *modes*—for Butler, the taking care of bodily precarity and the nonviolent resistance to violence—with which the piazza itself is organized. Certain Arendtians are right, then, to whisper among themselves about this problem: Arendt's insistence on a pure concept of the political, her predilection for a politics defined *justa propria principia*, which concentrates on the modes to the detriment of contents, risks leaving this problem in large part unresolved.

Butler distances herself from "those who will say that active bodies assembled on the street constitute a powerful and surging multitude, one that in itself constitutes a radical democratic event or action"; and she declares herself unwilling to endorse uprising multitudes who would regenerate politics with "the promising life force" of their mere action.[5] She prefers instead to join "a struggle to establish more sustaining conditions of livability in the face of systematically induced precarity and forms of racial destitution."[6] Hers is, therefore, a choice both of modes and of contents. In truth, even prior, such a choice concerns the name we give to the collective subject that enters and operates in the public space: *plurality* instead of *multitude* or *masses*, a term even more compromised. Indeed, our need, not only speculative, of defining as "democratic" only some "squares" and not others, some "spaces of appearance" and not others, cannot but pass through a dutiful reflection on this nomenclature.

Arendt occasionally uses—at times in a neutral sense, but mostly in a disparaging way—the word *multitude*, adopting it often as a synonym for *masses*, a concept on which she instead develops a wide and detailed analysis in her book on totalitarianism. Her basic thesis is that totalitarian movements find a fertile ground "wherever there are masses who for one reason or another have acquired the appetite for political organization."[7] At the time Arendt writes these words, in the initial years of the 1950s, the term masses already has a prodigious history behind it, a myriad of studies—sociological, psychological, and political—that describe the masses as an undifferentiated conglomerate of individuals who melt into one, single body. The phenomenon, Arendt notes, is proved by "the feeling of superfluousness" that is inherent to the masses, [8] that is, by that reduction of human plurality to a mass of superfluous human beings that, in her view, constitutes the darkest heart of totalitarianism and finds its definitive realization in the extermination camps.

The German *die Masse*, the Italian *massa*, and the corresponding *foule* in French, as well as *crowd* or *crowds* in English, have an interesting etymology. *Mass* derives from the Greek *maza*, meaning mix, as in the mix of dough combining flour, water, and oil for simple flatbread; this is not unlike the etymon of the French *foule* or Italian *folla*, which goes back to the Latin verb *fullare*, meaning to press, to squeeze, for instance, as in treading grapes or felting wool. Similar is the English *crowd*, which traces back to the Middle High German verb *kroten*—to press, to compact.[9] The concept underpinning this terminology denotes a conglomerate that, through the pressure of its components, becomes compact, undifferentiated, and uniform; that is, something whose substance is a single and homogeneous, though amorphous and mobile, unity that tends to be uncontainable. In the masses, in principle, individuality—and even more so uniqueness—vanishes into the indistinct unity of the collective subject.

In appearance, the word *multitude*, particularly in vogue today to exalt the insurgent crowds, avoids the idea of unity evoked by the masses and alludes instead to a molecular consistency. Plato, bitter enemy of democracy and champion of the entire, successive antidemocratic line, already gave the *demos* and the plebs the name of "the many" (*hoi polloi*) with obvious derogatory intent. A similar fate largely befalls the noun *multitude* in Latin texts, often used as a synonym for "plebeian" and "commoners," intended precisely in a derogatory sense. Although in the minority, we find, however, in ancient and modern authors, a different use of this very nomenclature, that is, a positive use of these same terms that, revealingly, end up calling forth the "people." Indeed, while *commoners* (Latin *vulgus*) maintains a negative value throughout the tradition, both the word *plebs/plebeian* (referring to a class that, let us not forget, in Rome has in the Gracchi its tribunes) and terms like *multitude, crowd, masses*, and, even more so, *the people*, appear in political treatises also with a positive valence.[10] These are essentially ambiguous terms: their value depends on the political perspective of the one who uses them, and, therefore, on the positive or negative valuation that each term gains in the different ideological and argumentative context. It is worth recalling that, contrary to Hobbes, Spinoza—who, not by chance, is appealed to by the current supporters of the uprising "multitudes"—uses *multitudo* in a positive and affirmative sense. The same can be said of the Marxist concept of "proletarian masses." The fact remains that, regardless of their derogatory or laudatory use, the concept of the "multitudes" as well as that of the "masses" denote a collective subject that tends to incorporate the individuality of the person, making it, if not superfluous, insignificant. With this type of nomenclature, we are, therefore, dealing with a viewpoint completely opposite to that in which the Arendtian category of plurality stands out, which, far from agglutinating individuals, exalts precisely the embodied uniqueness, distinctive and exhibitive, of those who compose it. Indeed, plurality's quality comes from the uniqueness of its political actors.

The rank of scholars who, in modern times, focus their attention on the masses is broad and varied. It includes authors like Gustave Le Bon, Sigmund Freud, Max Weber, Elias Canetti, and many others. Despite the different articulations of their approach or disciplinary perspective, they share the thesis that the phenomenology of the masses is structurally characterized by the "irrational" drives of individuals to merge into an amorphous collectivity. The obsession for the topic of the masses emerges in the final decades of the nineteenth century and then becomes dominant in the period between the two World Wars, a period defined, not by chance, by the relevant literature, as "the age of the masses," or rather "the age of the crowd" as we read in English texts. Actually, this consolidated rule of translating the German *die Masse* of Freud and Canetti, or the *foule* of Le Bon, with the English terms *crowd* or *crowds*, engenders a certain confusion. The very issue at stake, however, remains the same. Scholars more or less agree on the fact that, in this troubled age that comes face to face with totalitarianism, in addition to serving as a "conceptual tool for social scientists," the mass "was also the ideal slogan for politicians, and it was the chosen image for artists and writers, who all struggled to represent a society in flux and people in upheaval."[11] A sociological study from the 1920s provides, among the various definitions of *die Masse*, this one, then predominant: "a temporary association of people in a state of strong excitement (as ecstasy or panic), in which self-consciousness and higher spiritual faculties strongly regress (and without sign of any collective consciousness in the sense of a community)."[12]

Anticipating a topic certain to gain wide currency, already Gustave Le Bon, who published his pioneering text *The Psychology of Crowds* in 1895, writes that crowds (*foules*) are marked by feminine characteristics.[13] In other words, they are marked by that irrational and hysterical predisposition which, along with regressive, primitive, infantile, and animal-like attributes, will constitute the typical legacy of the phenomenon of the masses according to many of the subsequent critical studies. It is perhaps unnecessary to point out that, within the evident patriarchal prejudice of this framework, the qualification of the irrational and instinctual crowd as feminine functions as a perfect oppositional pole to the rational subject modeled on the masculine, which, not surprisingly, when it merges into the crowd, is feminized. It is, moreover, a well-known tendency to use female figures, like the famous French Marianne, to symbolize—in a positive way—the unity of the people and of the nation. For better or worse, in this type of albeit variegated imaginary, the feminine tends to represent unity, solidarity, and fusion or, at least, the emotional and passionate side of congregating in a collective subject; the masculine, as tradition dictates, is instead held to be more apt for evoking the notion of the individual subject, rational, civilized, and capable of controlling himself. More or less unsaid, the idea prevails that, just as women have need of a husband, likewise the feminized masses have need, or better still, yearn to surrender themselves to a leader, more or less virile, who dominates them. It is unnecessary to reiterate that we are here at the exact opposite of any political understanding of plurality, and especially of the Arendtian notion of plurality that, by exalting the acting in concert of unique beings, rescues the very idea of politics either from the grip of depersonalizing and fusional dynamics or from the grasp of vertical and virile patterns of power.

Among the thousands of texts dedicated to the subject of the masses in the twentieth century stands out, for its originality and voluminousness, the book *Crowds and Power* (German title: *Masse und Macht*) by Elias Canetti, published in 1960, but the fruit of a long elaboration lasting almost forty years. In this very complex work, Canetti examines the phenomenon of the crowd and classifies its various forms from multiple disciplinary perspectives, often resorting to metaphors and images that shed interesting light on his reflections. One of these images, rather frequent for that matter within the tradition, is that of the sea. Equating the sea with the crowd, he speaks of a movement of cohesion that entails "a yielding to others as though they were oneself, as though there were no strict division between oneself and them."[14] The image also allows Canetti to indulge his special passion for the auditory sphere, a specialty that makes him a particularly valuable author for the subject we are engaging with. Indeed, we read in *Crowds and Power*:

> The sea has a *voice*, which is very changeable and almost always audible. It is a voice which sounds like a thousand voices. . . . The sea never sleeps; by day and by night it makes itself heard, throughout years and decades and centuries. In its impetus and its rage, it brings to mind the one entity which shares these attributes in the same degree; that is, the crowd. But the sea has, in addition, the constancy which the crowd lacks. It is always there; it does not ooze away from time to time and disappear. To *remain* in existence is the greatest, though as yet fruitless desire of the crowd; and this desire is seen fulfilled in the sea.[15]

The most typical expression of the "voice of the crowd" is, however, according to Canetti, "the spontaneous and never quite unpredictable outcry, whose effect is enormous. It can express emotions of any kind; *which* emotions often matters less than their strength and variety and freedom of their sequence. It is they which give the crowd its 'feeling' space."[16] The most meaningful analyses of the phenomenology of the crowd and of its sonorous characteristics come, however, from the autobiographical writings of Canetti; to be precise, from the three books of memoir that, in the English edition, are collected in one copious volume under the title *The Memoirs of Elias Canetti*.[17]

In these memoirs, critiquing Le Bon and Freud for their abstract and prejudicial approach to a phenomenon that they know only in theory, from the outside, Canetti proudly declares instead to have done an empirical experiment on the crowd, to have known it from the inside: "I had unresistingly fallen prey to a crowd in Frankfurt for the first time," he confesses, "and since then I had never forgotten how *gladly* one falls prey to the crowd."[18] The decisive opportunity to be a part of the crowd, however, occurred a few years later for Canetti, on the memorable day of July 15, 1927, in Vienna, when he joined a massive demonstration of workers, during which the Palace of Justice was burned and a clash with the police left ninety dead. "I became a part of the crowd, I fully dissolved in it," he claims, recounting his Viennese experience and declaring that "since then, I have known quite precisely that I would not have to read a single word about the storming of the Bastille."[19] He further asserts, with a certain polemical attitude, that "the crowd needs no leader to form, notwithstanding all previous theories in this respect."[20] For Canetti, the "mimetic pathos," the emotional contagion that aggregates and moves the crowd, is entirely internal to the crowd itself.[21] That which he experiences is an autogenous crowd without a leader; the possible presence of speakers in the crowd, who group together a portion of it temporarily, is marginal and insignificant, according to Canetti.

"I heard a great deal," he writes, "there was always something to hear; most cutting of all were the boohs when the police fired into the throng and people fell. At such moments, the boohs were relentless, especially the female boohs, which could be made out distinctly"; "I felt as I were in a resonant wind," he adds, because "you *heard* something everywhere: there was something rhythmic in the air, an evil music. You could call it music, you felt elevated by it."[22] This acoustic experience in Vienna is indeed decisive for Canetti. After that, he declares with renewed pride, "I retained a sensitive ear for the voice of a crowd," and "it was only the Fifteenth of July that had opened my ears."[23] So crucial, for Canetti, is this opening wide of the ear that he develops a special predisposition for enjoying the sonority of the crowd, whether listening from the inside, from the outside, or from a distance. He recalls, in fact, his excitement in hearing the shouts that would come from the Rapid Stadium, a soccer field not far from his house, where matches were played on Sundays and holidays. "Throughout the six years that I lived in this room," he writes, "I missed no opportunity to listen to these sounds" and to receive in this way the "loud nourishment" by ear.[24]

Susan Sontag notes that "to give sovereignty to the ear is an obtrusive, consciously archaizing theme in Canetti's later work. Implicitly he is restating the archaic gap between Hebrew as opposed to Greek culture, ear culture as opposed to eye culture, and the moral versus the aesthetic."[25] Canetti himself claims to be more of a listener than an observer. His predilection for soundscapes, far from being a curious trait, turns into a cognitive specialty, particularly prolific and original. Indeed, it is worth reiterating that precisely this specialty makes him an interesting author with regard to the plethora of studies, often repetitive and verbose, dedicated to the subject of the crowd. This is all the more true when what is at stake, rather than the crowd itself, is the search for effective parameters in order to distinguish the crowd from plurality. Formulated as a question: Is there a sonorous difference between the voice of plurality and that of the masses? Is there an acoustically perceptible difference between their distinct phonospheres?

The voice of the crowd, as not only Canetti argues, manifests itself often with an outcry, like a thunderous ensemble of sounds, noises, clamors, screams, excited by their sinister rhythm, like an evil music "marked by a secret notation."[26] Yet it also manifests, and perhaps even more typically, as a voice composed of thousands of voices pronouncing words and singing in unison. And then the music of the masses becomes not only arcane and enthralling, but—reaching the maximum degree of fusion of collective emotional states—thrilling.

Judith Butler justly observes that "usually, we associate the event of everyone speaking the same thing at the same time with forms of fascism or other compulsory forms of conformity."[27] And she adds—with a certain, even more just concern—that, if "an assembled group were to yell out 'we the people,' as sometimes happens in the assembly of the Occupy Movement, it is a brief and transitory moment, one in which a single person speaks at the same time that others speak, and some unintended plural sounding results from that concerted plural action, that act spoken in common, with all the variations that repetition implies."[28] The argumentative context that Butler is grappling with, here, is that of her extensive reflection on the cases in which bodies assembled in the squares or demonstrating in the street pronounce the famous phrase "we the people" that appears in the Constitution of the United States. Her thesis is that, when vocalized by an interactive plurality, such an enunciation can "bring about the social plurality it names."[29] Quite clearly, Butler's intent is that of rethinking the concept of "the people" in terms

5: The Voice of the Masses

of plurality rather than as homogeneous unity. However, the case of a plurality that, vocalizing "we the people," speaks in unison makes the endeavor particularly arduous. Especially since, as Butler wells knows, in unison, in squares, and during demonstrations, voices are often raised that chant slogans or sing. Butler writes:

> Even when a crowd speaks together, they have to gather in close enough proximity to hear each other's voice, to pace each person's own vocalization, to achieve rhythm and harmony to a sufficient degree, and so to achieve a relation both auditory and corporeal with those with whom some signifying action or speech act is undertaken. . . . Temporal seriality and coordination, bodily proximity, auditory range, coordinated vocalization—all of these constitute essential dimensions of assembly and demonstration. . . . Sounds are but one way to signify in common—singing, chanting, declaring, beating drums or pots, or pounding against a prison or separation wall.[30]

There is, indeed, a just concern behind this eloquent phrasing of Butler: the phenomenon of people that recite or speak in unison evokes the phenomenology of the crowd, not that of plurality. It evokes a phonosphere that is typical of the sonority of the masses, not of plurality. Canetti is perfectly aware of this, and Arendt perceives this too, although not with as refined an ear.

Arendt briefly focuses her attention on the vocal masses, in her book *On Revolution*. It happens in a passage—mostly unwelcome to her commentators—in which she describes the dramatic theater of the poor and hungry who rose up shouting "Bread!" during the French Revolution. It was certainly not a plurality, argues Arendt, but rather a multitude:

> only in the mere numerical sense. Rousseau's image of a "multitude" . . . united in one body and driven by one will was an exact description of what they actually were, for what urged them on was the quest for bread and the cry for bread will always be uttered with one voice. In so far as we all need bread, we are indeed all the same and may as well unite into one body. It is by no means merely a matter of misguided theory that the French concept of *le peuple* has carried, from its beginning, the connotation of a multiheaded monster, a mass that moves as one body and acts as though possessed by

one will; and if this notion has spread to the four corners of the earth, it is because of its obvious plausibility under conditions of abject poverty.[31]

The tone can seem contemptuous, but one must not forget that, in Arendtian terms, plurality is incompatible with any fusion of a multitude in a single body dramatically vocalized in unison by people who shout "Bread!" And it is good, moreover, to recall that the popular revolts of the hungry are not a novelty on the French—and European—scene but rather characterize the so-called "bread riots" over the entire course of the eighteenth century.[32] In light of Arendt's concept of politics, which intentionally excludes the sphere of bodily needs and life's necessities, that she does not recognize in the Parisian crowd shouting "Bread!" the political action of plurality therefore causes little surprise. Arendt has, furthermore, plausible reasons for mistrusting every word or phrase or slogan or song uttered in unison. The image of the so-called "choreographed masses," who simultaneously move and shout out and sing as one body—so dear to Nazi aesthetics—cannot but arouse horror and disgust in a German Jewish woman who had experienced and studied the totalitarian phenomenon.

Singing is notoriously one of the most typical and moving expressions of the phonosphere of the crowd. And it is, in a certain sense, its most intense and peculiar auditory emission. As if, when individuals sing in unison, they melted together through the immersion in a collective, deindividualized voice—a pleasurable immersion in the sonority of a mystical body that incorporates their singular body, which is thus dislocated in a dimension of *ex-stasis*. With more or less intensity, depending on the historical circumstances of conflict or war, this is particularly evident in the case of crowds singing the national anthem to consolidate the unity, if not the homogeneity, of the nation. One of the most important scholars of fascist masses and racist culture, George Mosse, has observed that France's "Marseillaise" was the first national anthem written in march time; soon other countries began to sing the national anthem in contagious and warlike rhythms, intended to evoke the myth of blood sacrifice for the life of the nation.[33] Obviously, in its historical and geopolitical detail, the subject is very complex and would deserve an in-depth analysis. One can, however, try to shed a little light on it by rereading

5: The Voice of the Masses

a few enthralling pages of a novel by Émile Zola, another author endowed with a particularly sensitive ear for the sonority of the masses.

In his novel *The Fortune of the Rougons*, Zola describes a crowd on the march singing the "Marseillaise." The crowd is composed of patriots from the republican uprising against the 1851 coup d'état of Louis-Napoléon Bonaparte, patriots with whom Zola sympathizes and whose ardor he exalts, emphasizing the acoustic power of their singing in unison. In the scene in the novel that begins the description, we encounter two young lovers who, while walking "in the beautiful winter moonlight" of the Provençal countryside, perceive a muffled noise coming from behind the hills; but little by little the sound increases and becomes similar to the "footsteps of an army on the march."[34] "Then amidst the continuous growing rumble," writes Zola, "one detected the shouts of a crowd, strange rhythmical blasts as of a hurricane. One could even have fancied they were the thunderclaps of a rapidly approaching storm. . . . Suddenly a dark mass appeared at the turn of the road, and then the 'Marseillaise' burst forth, formidable, sung as with avenging fury." The text continues, narrating how the crowd descended the slope "with a superb, irresistible stride," a torrent of thousands of men, "whose songs ever helped to swell the roar of this human tempest." "The 'Marseillaise' filled the atmosphere as if blown through enormous trumpets by giant mouths, which cast it, vibrating with a brazen clang, into every corner of the valley." Zola insists on the echo of the natural landscape: "the roar of the populace thus rolled on in sonorous waves," he writes, and the "countryside awoke with a start—quivering like a beaten drum resonant to its very entrails and repeating with each and every echo the passionate notes of the national song." The description dwells particularly on the grandeur of the acoustic phenomenon, on how the natural landscape and the marching crowd join together in voicing a formidable song in unison. There is no respite in the auditory flow: the entire valley resounds as if a sole voice were expressing the unity of the "compact mass of invincible strength," in which is fused the "swarming, roaring stream" of the crowd in revolt. Even though each individual that makes up this crowd sings with a unique voice, their individual voices melt into a formidable vocal mass. And it is precisely this vocality, which vibrates in unison, that testifies to the collective experience of dissolving into a "compact mass." In a few pages,

Zola, with an acoustic sensitivity that equals that of Canetti, manages to give an account of the phonosphere of the masses in an exciting and perfect way. In addition to anticipating some of the fundamental themes of the phenomenology of the masses, which Le Bon, Freud, Canetti, and many others will debate, Zola's text has the merit of framing it explicitly and emphatically in vocal terms. Perhaps no other author provides as memorable a description of the singing voice of the crowd. It is quite clearly a specific type of crowd. The national anthem, the warlike rhythm of the "Marseillaise"—not to mention its violent lyrics—give to this voice that sings in unison a special significance, historic and patriotic. National anthems, for that matter, have precisely the function of producing and giving vocal substance to the unity of the nation, a specific form of unity in which the individual voices mix and blend together. Zola does not narrate the sonority of the masses in general, but rather that of the peculiar crowd that is linked to the phenomenon of the nation, in insurgent form, moreover, and with arms in hand. The suggestive rhetoric of his prose reveals this explicitly. The emphasis on the natural landscape that participates in the song succeeds in stressing the harmony of the sonorous performance. Indeed, at the center of the scene, there is, here, a vocal crowd that is structurally—one could even say "naturally"—harmonic.

Fictional writers are often a great resource, if not a veritable treasure, for thematizing the crowd in terms of vocality. This is, among others, the case with Boris Pasternak, novelist and poet of an extraordinary ear who has the misfortune of living under a totalitarian regime in Bolshevik Russia, where his writings, starting with the famous novel *Doctor Zhivago*, are subject to persecution because they do not conform to the regime's ideology. In this very novel, Pasternak describes a crowd of people in revolt, "pouring in a torrent" as they march in the streets of Moscow in November 1905, and who, after having sung other hymns in unison, eventually sing the "Marseillaise." "Then," writes the author, "a man who had been walking backwards at the head of the procession, singing and conducting with his cap," stopped conducting and turned around; "the singing broke off in disorder," continues Pasternak, "now you could hear the crunch of innumerable footsteps on the frozen pavement."[35] Although brief, in acoustic terms, the sequence is extraordinary. The passage from singing in unison to the sound of footsteps on the pavement describes with particular effectiveness the splitting apart of an emotionally compact unity into a sonority of a different type: mechanical, so to speak, and distributed through the multiplicity of shoes that brush against the frozen ground. One could speak of passing from the crowd to the multitude. In the breaking-off of the song, the crowd does not just lose its voice temporarily, but loses it in the form most apt to express its fusion in a single vocal body, such that the sound of steps that follows is a kind of dispersion of this unity. Singing in unison acoustically reveals the fusional nucleus of the crowd, its energy and vitality. The sound of steps on the pavement disperses these, as if it were a silence, a suspension, the auditory trace of a crowd that marches on but that is dramatically lacking the glue of vocality.

6

The Voice of Plurality

IN THE ESSAY "The Hungarian Revolution and Totalitarian Imperialism," Hannah Arendt reports on a singular and moving episode. In Moscow in 1946, Boris Pasternak arrived in a crowded hall for a reading of his poetry. Apparently, Arendt notes, it was the poet's only public appearance under the totalitarian regime; after all his years of silence, he was known only as the translator of Shakespeare and Goethe into Russian. Pasternak "read from his poems, and as he was reading an old poem the paper slipped from his hand; then a voice from the hall began to recite the poem from memory; from several corners of the hall, other voices joined in, and the recitation of the poem ended, interrupted, in a chorus."[1] Commenting on the episode, Arendt says that, to her knowledge, this is the only anecdote attesting that totalitarian domination had not yet been victorious in Russia, and thus "it is undoubtedly of great significance." Pasternak is a dissident author, and, in joining with him to recite one of his poems by heart, the Moscow audience displays an obvious complicity with his political stance. They share his position and make apparent that they do.

There is, however, an aspect of the episode, its vocal development, that goes beyond this effect of complicity. There is, in other words, a sonority that significantly weaves together the plot threads of the entire story. The protagonists of this act of resistance to totalitarianism are single voices, or

6: The Voice of Plurality

rather, to say it in the Arendtian lexicon, they are a plurality of unique voices. Their vocal performance hinders the very idea of totalitarian domination or, to put it again in Arendt's words, the "perfect totalitarian government where all men," by melting into a mass, "have become 'One Man.'"[2] On the other hand—and this is exactly the most interesting and problematic aspect of the anecdote—in reciting together a poem from memory, the plural, reciting voices become here a chorus that declaims in unison. Or rather, they produce the typical form of vocal expression that characterizes the masses. The case of a plurality that recites in unison is interesting because it directly challenges the assumption that the voice of plurality and the voice of the masses are expressions of different and opposed collective subjects. That is, that they are two essentially distinct political phonospheres. If investigated in its auditory storyline, the anecdote confronts us with a sort of paradox: it recounts an extraordinary case in which the effect of speaking in unison not only does not compact plurality into a mass but, on the contrary, exalts it.

Unexpected, unplanned, spontaneous, the choir consists of unique voices that progressively join in reciting the poem. The performance develops according to a precise temporal sequence. At the beginning, there is the voice of Pasternak; then, after a second of silence in which the paper slips from his hand, another voice intervenes continuing the interrupted vocalization; finally, without interruption, other voices join together in the choral recitation. The poem is recited in unison, but the most relevant element, in the dynamic of this choral performance—or rather, the element that makes it a political performance—is not the typical fusional effect of speaking in unison, but rather the adding, one after the other, of singular voices. Put another way, the voices unite with the choir as unique voices and, independently of the effect of reciting in chorus, remain plural. Plural indeed they are, in Arendt's understanding, and therefore free, resistant, political, antitotalitarian. Complicit, first of all, because relational; and relational to such an extent as to spontaneously share the vocalization of the poem, making of it the political plot of the event.

To tell the truth, commenting on the anecdote, Arendt does not pay particular attention to the vocal dynamic of the event. The vocabulary and the conceptual grid of her entire political speculation provide us, however, an ideal speculative ear for tuning into the extraordinary phonosphere of the anecdote. Above all, we are dealing here with the performance of unique, embodied voices, in corporeal and vocal relation in a shared space, whose plurality contrasts, as Arendt often repeats, the very idea of totalitarian domination. Even though these voices recite in unison, in the context of the anecdote's phenomenology and its valence as a political act, they remain unique and plural; they resist and demonstrate their resistance to the totalitarian regime because they are plural; better yet, they suddenly experience the public happiness of attuning themselves as plural. It is plurality itself, in the form of a particular sonority, that opposes here the hold of totalitarianism, acquiring an affirmative, creative, and springlike quality. As if the event of a surging democracy in the Moscow hall, sudden and unexpected, invaded the totalitarian space vocally. As if these voices, by reverberating in the hall, produced the auditory emotion of a democracy experienced in its nascent stage. Indeed, something unforeseeable happens in Moscow, a veritable political event: Pasternak's reading provides the opportunity for the Moscow hall to regenerate as an acoustic space for the auditory expression of a surging democracy incarnated by unique voices that recite chorally. In a previous book of mine, by grappling with the issue of acoustic space, I have spoken of "a politics of voices," a politics "where the speakers, no matter what they say, communicate first of all their vocalic uniqueness and the echo of a resonance as the essential prerequisites of verbal communication."[3] The event in the Moscow hall has, nevertheless, a singularity of its own. At stake, here, is the act of an interactive plurality that expresses its ontological and relational status through the physical uniqueness of single, embodied voices that, as such, in the choral recitation—uttered in unison, but in a unison that neither englobes them nor melts them into a unity—not only resist but generate a common space of interaction. And in so doing, they perhaps experience the public emotion of an unforeseen but no less familiar happiness.

One could say, with good reason, that their choral performance is harmonic. And yet, it is worth stressing, a harmony very different from that of the crowd singing the "Marseillaise" described by Zola. Not just because of the warlike rhythms, the marching feet, or other ambient and emotional sonorities, fusional and ecstatic, that insist on a phonosphere completely

6: The Voice of Plurality

incomparable with that which vibrates in the Moscow hall. But also, and especially, because of the issue that the Moscow hall raises in the form of paradox. For a plurality to recite or sing in unison is indeed an exception, an extraordinary case. It is worth recalling the clarifications, rightly worried, of Judith Butler regarding the phenomenon of "political squares" that occasionally speak or sing or recite slogans in unison, but that, normally are nevertheless characterized by the resonance of plural voices that say different words, of people who speak to each other, singularly or in groups. As a matter of fact, within the soundscape of plurality, the speaking in unison is an exception, something disturbing; while, symptomatically, the simultaneous and diffuse articulation of different words is the rule. Which would lead one to suppose that the voice of plurality, when it makes itself heard in its average form, resembles more a cacophony than a harmony or, as Roland Barthes would say, resembles a kind of rustle (*bruissement*). In fact, even though Barthes's suggestion is valuable, we should eventually find a specific term to designate this sonority of plural voices that simultaneously pronounce different words, yet do not produce a cacophony. And, obviously, we should look for a term ductile enough to even include the harmonic sonority of a plurality that recites or sings in unison yet is not a harmony. Many elements suggest that we call it *pluriphony*.

The first and explicit purpose of this neologism is to give a specific name to the voice of plurality as distinct from the voice of the masses, and opposed to it. On a lexical level, the tradition does not help us much. While the literature and essays on the sonority of crowds can rely on a conspicuous number of texts, the bibliography on vocal pluralities is indeed scarce. Fortunately, the exception, however, is again Elias Canetti, whose sensitive ear, already trained on the phonosphere of the masses, is capable of attuning itself to the voice of plurality too.

In his autobiographical novel, *The Voices of Marrakesh*, Canetti tells of a peculiar auditory experience. While walking through the Jewish quarter of the city, he hears a thin, high-pitched noise that sounds at first like crickets, gradually growing louder: he thinks of "an aviary full of birds," but soon discovers it is children. The strange noise comes from a school. Hundreds of tiny little children sit crammed together; "in groups of three or four they rocked violently backwards and forwards, reciting in high-pitched voices: 'Aleph. Beth. Gimel.' The little black heads darted rhythmically to and fro; one of them was always the most zealous, his movements the most vehement; and in his mouth the sounds of the Hebrew alphabet rang out like a decalogue in the making."[4] This is not the only acoustic experience that Canetti encounters in Marrakesh during his visit of a few weeks. For Canetti, hungry for listening and always in search of "loud nourishment,"[5] the city is an aural space, all the more fascinating since he understands neither Arabic nor any of the Berber languages spoken by the population. He wants those sounds to "affect" him for what they are, without the knowledge of their meaning or the understanding of the language diminishing their power.[6] To capture in words the sonic essence of Marrakesh, Canetti recounts different acoustic impressions that strike his ear, coming from a flow of sound in which the voices of humans and those of animals blend with the various noises, screams, and cries of the populous city. Canetti describes the cries of blind beggars who, weaving "acoustic arabesques" around the sound "Allah, Allah, Allah," in the market, repeated a hoarse litany "audible long way off."[7] In the central square, conversely, "a small, brown bundle on the ground consisting not even of a voice but of a single sound"—a man of whom Canetti can see neither the face nor the mouth—continuously emitted the sound *e-e-e-e-e*. "Perhaps it had no tongue with which to form the 'l' of 'Allah' and to it the name of God was abbreviated to 'e-e-e-e-e,'" writes Canetti, but this single sound expressed, with unparalleled diligence and persistence, the reality of a unique existence at the limit of the living.[8]

The shrieks of poor children asking for food in front of restaurants complete the auditory landscape, which is, however, also composed of animal cries and noises of every sort. Even though the human voice remains the main object of his acoustic experience in Marrakesh, Canetti listens to it as an element of a broader and more varied polyphony. Evoking this abundance of sounds and heterogeneous, acoustic impressions, his account aims first and foremost at celebrating "the voice as an agency that releases language from the constraints of the symbolic order," that is, that frees language from the semantic dimension.[9] In the works of Canetti, the interest in the phonic materiality of language, to the detriment of the semantic dimension, is a

6: The Voice of Plurality

recurring theme. He repeatedly argues that the sonority of speech, its consisting of sounds emitted by the human voice, is particularly effective when he happens to hear a foreign language that he does not understand. Because it is distinct from the semantic code of language, the acoustic phenomenology of speech, all the more perceptible if we do not know the language, has a reality all its own that signifies beyond the signification: "Canetti is not simply interested in voice as a supplement of language; he is particularly fascinated by those moments when this supplement stands alone—the experience of voice unaccompanied by understanding, the encounter with pure voice."[10] Tellingly, Canetti claims to be more of a listener than an observer; his is a human ear wide open to acoustic events. "The voice for Canetti stands for irrefutable presence," notes Susan Sontag; for him, "to affirm that one hears means the one hears what must be heard."[11] Even inarticulate sounds, at the limit of the living, like the *e-e-e-e-e* emitted by the brown bundle on the ground, stand like the irrefutable presence of a singular life.

Canetti's attention to the auditory element gives important results wherever he describes the phonosphere of the masses, either in *Crowds and Power* or, especially, in his autobiographical writings. His sensitivity to the acoustic sphere is even more valuable, however, when it is attuned to the uniqueness of every voice and to the voice of plurality. Beyond his interest in the sonority of entire landscapes and environments, what matters most is indeed his predilection for the auditory dimension of language, understood as expression of a human vocality, singular and plural, closely tied to discourse and speech. Attracted by this vocality, which conveys but exceeds the semantic dimension of language, Canetti listens to the voice and delights, precisely, in its capacity for excess. One thus understands why he privileges the situations in which, listening to the sounds emitted by someone who speaks an unknown language, he can enjoy the pure phonic dimension without the order of meanings interfering in his listening. Well exemplified by his enjoyment of children's voices in Marrakesh, in Canetti's texts the subject is frequent and almost obsessive. For example, speaking of Backenroth, a classmate who speaks Yiddish, of whom he describes the twittering "soft voice, strange and extraordinarily tender," Canetti confesses: "when I noticed him talking, I automatically drew closer, in order to hear his voice, though I understood nothing."[12] Even more telling is his collaboration with his friend Ibby Gordon on the German translation of poems that she writes in her mother tongue, Hungarian. Ibby enjoyed reciting them, recounts Canetti: "I always wanted to hear them in Hungarian first, and then, when I was enchanted by their sound, we attempted to translate them"; "if I had not first heard them in a language I had no inkling of, they might have meant nothing to me."[13] The enchantment of the sound—a well known and essential aspect of poetic composition that every translator must obviously take into account—becomes for Canetti more powerful and even eloquent when it offers itself to his ear as pure vocality. Whether in regard to poetry or simply spoken discourse, not understanding a word is precisely what strengthens to the highest degree the auditory and musical dimension of language, an object of acoustic enjoyment for Canetti from early childhood, when he hears his parents speak in German, a mysterious language that he does not yet know. It is plausible that Canetti's acoustic sensitivity to the sound of language is due to the experience of the different languages with which he comes into contact during his childhood. Born in Bulgaria in 1905, into a family of Sephardic Jews who speak Ladino, he grows up in a multicultural environment where Bulgarian and Romanian (in addition to the German spoken by his parents) are everyday tongues. He learns English as a child while living in Manchester, and at school he masters with ease other ancient and modern languages. Revealingly, during early childhood, the particular fascination of German, secret language of his parents, attracts him both on the acoustic level as well as on that of writing. Sound and writing become the magic key for discovering the secret of the unknown language.

In the first book of his *Memoirs*, tellingly entitled *The Tongue Set Free*, Canetti recounts how, as a child, he was subjugated by the voice of his father, who, accompanied by his mother on the piano, on holiday evenings would sing *Lieder* by Schubert or Loewe: "I did not understand German, at the time, but the song was heart-rending."[14] But he also recounts how he was attracted by the small letters printed on the pages of the *Neue Freie Presse*, the German newspaper that his father read every morning. To little Elias, who does not yet know how to read, the father explains that the important thing about the newspaper is precisely the small letters he points at with his finger. "Soon I would learn them myself, he said, arousing within me an unquenchable yearning for letters."[15] This unquenchable yearning has a dramatic consequence, which Canetti recounts in a famous episode from the same book. His older cousin Laurica, returning from school, shows him a notebook that contains the letters of the alphabet, written in blue ink, but forbids the little boy from touching them. The same sequence of events goes on for days, with Laurica refusing her cousin contact with the letters in the notebook, despite his supplications: until, exasperated, Elias takes up an axe and rushes toward his cousin, shouting, "Agora vo matar a Laurica!"—"Now I'm going to kill Laurica!"[16] His grandfather stops him, fortunately, but Canetti will never forget how the fascination of the letters of the alphabet was able to subjugate him to the point of transforming him into a murderer. Dramatic as it is, this episode sheds interesting light on the page Canetti dedicates to the twittering children in the school in Marrakesh. He recounts how, while he was in the middle of this pluriphonic tempest, the teacher called one of the little pupils to him, holding a page of the primer up in front of him in such a way that Canetti could see it too. Then the teacher pointed "to Hebraic syllables in quick succession, switching from line to line, backwards and forwards across the page at random; I was not to think that the boy had learned it by heart and was reciting blind, without reading."[17] Next the proud teacher called, one by one, the other pupils and repeated the ceremony with each of them. "For the entire duration of this proceeding, the din continued unabated, and the Hebraic syllables fell like raindrops in the raging sea of the school."[18] The method of the teacher, who switches from line to line, randomly pointing his finger at the syllables across the page, has a precise goal: the attention does not focus on what the text means, on the meanings of the words and of the story, but rather on the alphabet and on the syllables, in both their phonic and written expression. In the mouths of the children, who vocalize it with the plurality of their different voices, each unique and irreplaceable, in the school in Marrakesh, language vibrates in its elemental sounds, corresponding to the signs on the page. While Canetti abandons himself to the acoustic enjoyment of the sound of language—which gives itself here in its pure form because it is decomposed in its pure phonemes, and hence radically freed from the weight of meaning—he can thus also satisfy his unquenchable yearning for the letters.

Canetti's account of his acoustic enjoyment of the voices of the children, who, at the Hebrew school in Marrakesh, produce a feast of sounds, finds an interesting echo in an essay by Roland Barthes on the rustle of language, published in France a few years later.[19] Barthes recounts how, while watching Michelangelo Antonioni's film on China (*Chung Kuo-Cina*, 1973), he suddenly experienced the rustle of language at the end of a sequence showing,

> in a village street, some children, leaning against a wall, reading aloud, each one a different book to himself but all together; that rustled in the right way, like a machine that works well; the meaning was doubly impenetrable to me, by my not knowing Chinese and by the blurring of these simultaneous readings; but I was hearing, in a kind of hallucinated perception (so intensely was it receiving all the subtlety of the scene), I was hearing the music, the breath, the tension, the application, in short something like a *goal*. Is that all it takes—just speak all at the same time in order to make language rustle, in the rare fashion, stamped with delectation, that I have been trying to describe? No, of course not; the auditory scene requires an erotics (in the broadest sense of the term), the élan, or the discovery, or the simple accompaniment of an emotion: precisely what was contributed by the countenances of the Chinese children.[20]

Just as the proper functioning of a machine—for example, the engine of a car—is acoustically perceived as a rustle, the same thing occurs with the rustle of language: "the rustle is the noise of what is working well." It is a particular sound that, paradoxically, according to Barthes, denotes a limit-noise and has no noise; "to rustle is to make audible the very evaporation of noise: the tenuous, the blurred, the tremulous are received as the signs of an auditory annulation." "The rustle of language," adds Barthes, "forms a utopia: that of a music of meaning." It is a music made of an auditory fabric in which the semantic apparatus is made unreal and yet does not disappear. It is a music that allows the phonic, metric, and vocal signifier to display all of its sumptuosity, "without meaning being brutally dismissed, dogmatically foreclosed, in short castrated." Put another way, the rustle of language does not abandon the horizon of meaning, of the semantic. "Meaning, undivided, impenetrable, unnamable" is instead "posited in the distance like a mirage,"

6: The Voice of Plurality

making the vocal exercise into a double landscape furnished with "a background"; "but instead of the music of the phonemes being the 'background' of our messages (as happens in our poetry), meaning would now be the vanishing point of delectation." At the conclusion of this brief essay, Barthes states that he imagines himself something like the ancient Greeks, as Hegel described them: they interrogated "passionately, uninterruptedly, the rustle of branches, of springs, of winds, in short, the shudder of Nature, in order to perceive in it the design of an intelligence. And I—it is the shudder of meaning I interrogate, listening to the rustle of language, that language which for me, modern man, is my Nature."

Even though he seems to share Canetti's passion for acoustic experience, Barthes is not interested in the variety of soundscapes composed of human and inhuman voices, in the mixture of heterogeneous sounds that includes vocal emissions. He is, rather, explicitly interested in language and, more precisely, in that particular sonority of language that he calls "rustle": "the sound of plural delectation" within the act of uttering words, as he writes. Tellingly, the formula of "plural delectation" could be applied to the children of the Hebrew school of Marrakesh that Canetti talks about. Here, as in the case of the Chinese children described by Barthes, it is the sonority of language, chanted by a plurality of voices, that delights the children themselves as well as Canetti who listens to them. The vocal performance, the rustle, involves ears and throats in "an erotics" of plural delectation that vibrates with a special emotion. In this plural vocality, nevertheless, a certain shudder of meaning, along with the active and interrelated participation in the performance, makes itself heard: a shudder that is all the more perceptible to the ear if the language is unknown to the listener, as both Canetti and Barthes affirm. As if plurality expressed itself in the form of a pluriphony neither harmonic nor cacophonic—despite the simultaneity of voices that pronounce different words—in which the resounding element signifies the plurality itself and its delectation. As if the phonosphere of plurality manifested itself in the basic form of nonfusional acoustic relation, the precondition and announcement of any collective subject that can claim to be plural.

It is worth lingering again on the extraordinary capacity of Canetti for exploring the full range of the vocal sphere, thematizing not only the sonority of the masses, but also the uniqueness of each voice, always inserted by him in a relational and plural context characterized by distinction rather than by fusion.

Canetti is well aware that the chirping sound of the children in the school in Marrakesh is produced by single voices, each unique and different from every other. What strikes his ear is precisely a pluriphonic vocality whose expressivity prevails over the semantic. And it is worth stressing that this pure vocality, on which Canetti and Barthes, not by chance, insist, far from facilitating a fusion of singular voices, exalts their plurality. In this sense, one should recognize, in both Canetti and Barthes, the merit not only of having been able to describe the voice of plurality, but also, and especially, of having provided a useful criterion for individuating it and, even more valuably, of having encouraged us to attune our ear to the various situations in which plurality, no matter where, manifests itself, sings, or speaks. In other words, texts like these encourage our ear to acoustically perceive plurality even when we happen to listen to "political squares" that speak a language unknown to us. And it encourages us, even prior, to distinguish the voice of plurality in the inevitable noise produced by the interaction of many people who speak to each other or in groups, at the same time and in the same space. Which is precisely what normally occurs within the plurality's phonosphere.

On the other hand, at least on the empirical level, it is also true that many of us are not entirely lacking a sense of hearing capable of attuning itself to the sonority of collective subjects. Even if we do not possess an exquisite hearing like that of Canetti, either by nature or by experience, many of us have, in fact, an ear quite sensitive to the voice of plurality when we hear it in the squares that Butler describes; just as many of us have, in general, an ear easily moved—and dangerously thrilled—by crowds that sing in unison. And, in all probability, a number of us are even able to distinguish the tone of public happiness, which resonates in the participative music of plural "assemblies," from the menacing tone of violence and aggression that instead vibrates in the vitalistic music of certain vocal crowds.

Butler notes that "the idea of bodies on the street together gives leftists a bit of a thrill, as if power were being taken back, taken away, assumed and incorporated in some way that portends democracy." "I understand that thrill," she admits.[21] It is perhaps the thrill that takes her back to the years of her adolescence, to her first experiences of participating in political demonstrations in which bodies come together and count. But, more generally, it is that thrill, not necessarily of the Left, that regularly seizes whoever is involved or finds herself in the presence of a collective subject in mobilization, as if it were the very contact with the collective subject, no matter whether ascribable to the phenomenology of the crowd or that of plurality, that "naturally" provokes such a state of excitement. Which does not mean, as Butler rightly observes, that the revolutionary imaginary—with its entire corollary of struggles, uprisings, and the democratic ideals it contains—is not crucial in giving leftists a bit of a thrill at the idea of assembled bodies taking to the street. But it does mean, at least, that, if on the one hand it is important to register, with a certain disturbing preoccupation, the spontaneity of our emotional state in the face of any corporeal and vocal expression, collective in form, on the other hand it is perhaps even more important to reflect on the diverse range of emotions—fusional or participative, identitarian or inclusive—triggered by the different types of these forms. That it be first and foremost social psychology that takes charge of the work is obvious. Narrators with a highly trained ear, like Canetti, touch upon the issue, however, at a critical point, when they describe the emotional effect of these collective forms in terms of vocality and acutely distinguish their phonospheres. Paraphrasing Canetti, Susan Sontag has rightly observed that "the ear is the attentive sense, humbler, more passive, more immediate, less discriminating than the eye."[22] When you know how to listen to it, plurality has a distinct sound. A pluriphonic rustle.

As a good narrator, Canetti often insists in his writings on the phenomenon of vocal uniqueness, considering it an essential element. The uniqueness of each voice, expression of an embodied singularity that bursts into the general order of speech, is not only mentioned by him several times but described in detail with particular precision. For example, of the voice of Thomas Marek, a paralytic friend who would read, turning the pages of the book with his tongue, Canetti points out that "his voice sounded breathy, as if coming from deep inside him, it gave color and space to his greeting."[23] For others, including famous writers like Hermann Broch or Robert Musil, he depicts the vocal inflection and way of speaking, the tonality and the accent.

In short, there is not a character, fictitious or real, in the narrative works of Canetti of whom he does not describe the quality of voice, searching—as much as possible through a soundless medium like that of writing—to acoustically render the uniqueness of it.

The muteness of writing becomes an even more obsessive problem for Canetti when it comes to theatrical works. He writes a few plays and, while waiting—often futilely!—for them to be staged, he reads them to a small audience of friends and acquaintances. About his *Comedy of Vanity*, he declares: "to appreciate the *Comedy*, one had to *hear* it; it was based on what I have called acoustic masks; each character was clearly demarcated from all the others by choice of words, intonation and rhythm, and there was no way of showing this in writing. My intentions could be made clear only by a complete reading."[24] During this reading, Canetti strives to imitate the voice of each of the protagonists of his play, so that they acoustically differ from each other, in order to make all the characters "recognizable by their voices."[25] The uniqueness of each voice, paradoxically, makes itself thus heard in the sole voice of Canetti who imitates them. Although it remains singular, his voice becomes plural or, at least, undertakes the impossible feat of reproducing the human plurality of voices.

Sincerely admiring Robert Musil, Canetti declares that he especially appreciates in Musil's work his conception of individuals as distinct fields of knowledge: "the sterile notion that any single theory might be applicable to all people was utterly alien to him. Each individual was distinct and different."[26] This is true also for Canetti: sharing Musil's attention to uniqueness as anti-universalistic dispositive, he strives, first and foremost, to render the corporeal materiality of uniqueness in terms of vocal expression. His narrative texts are inhabited by subjectivities that vocally communicate the uniqueness and the plurality of a structurally relational human condition.

There is an evident correspondence of themes, a resonance of concepts, an affinity between the narrative texts of Canetti and Roland Barthes's essay on the rustle of language. The rustle of language, affirms Barthes, as it is once again worth repeating, consists "of the sound of plural delectation" within the act of uttering words. This can also be applied to the children of the Hebrew school in Marrakesh. And it is no coincidence that, in addition to exalting the

6: The Voice of Plurality

sonority at the expense of the semantic factor, both scenes have children as protagonists. Perceived in its pure phonic substance, the interactive context is joyously plural.

Here, however, we are not at all in the Greek *agorà* imagined by Arendt, or in "the political squares" described by Butler, much less in the Moscow hall where the voices improvise a chorus. We are, resoundingly, in the initial phase of every human being's life, childhood. In a certain sense, birth is still near, and, in an even more significant sense, the plurality that vocally expresses itself here is not yet political. Childhood acts as a bridge and announces in advance, so to speak, the phonic signature of a democracy to come. As if the archetypal voice of plurality were precisely the voice of a spring, pure and full of hope, vibrant and joyful, happy with its plural being. A voice whose emotional manifestation, far from consisting of the pleasure of dissolving into one body, comes instead from the enjoyment of plurality, of its corporeal and vocal relations. As if surging democracy had a sound that revocalizes, every time anew and as adults too, the nascent and generative happiness of beginning.

SCHERZO Crowds with a Cellphone

7
Crowds with a Cellphone

THE SCENE TAKES PLACE in Teramo, Italy, in January 2019, and has as a protagonist Matteo Salvini, leader of the Lega Party and (at that time) minister of the interior, serving also as deputy prime minister, who meets the crowd. But it could have other political leaders as protagonists, Italian and foreign, like Luigi Di Maio, Matteo Renzi, Barack Obama, Hillary Clinton, Donald Trump, Vladimir Putin, or still others. That is, it could take place anywhere there is a popular political leader, capable of increasing their success as a media figure through a continuous and astute use of social media. The party and the ideology, tellingly, have little importance here. What counts is fixing our gaze on the extemporaneous relation between the crowd and the leader in the age of the personalization of politics and the smartphone.

Let us hear from the Italian writer Ivan Carozzi who, in an article for *Il Post*, thus describes the scene in Teramo, defining it as exemplary of "the connection between power, crowds, and technology":

> Salvini comes out into the street and finds, on his right and left, two wings of a crowd controlled by a double cordon of police. All these people are squeezed into a line waiting for a selfie. Salvini is perfectly prepared, given that the same scene has probably been repeating itself everywhere for some time. Salvini has developed an expertise in regard to the selfie and has become a true maestro of the ceremony. He gesticulates and gives directions on technique in a loud voice, not without a relaxed peremptoriness; he takes

advantage of the moment to crack a joke about the "Left," then asks these people pressed together in a line to prepare their cellphones. He actually says: "Prepare your cellphones." Then he approaches the first group, indicates where to proceed once the photo is taken, and takes the phone directly from each person's hand, with a certain brutality, then focuses, smiles, and shoots. He even gets annoyed with those who arrive with their cellphone not "prepared." There are those who approach and whisper something into his ear. Meanwhile, the police officers remain close by so that the selfie ceremony takes place without incident.[1]

In the video of the event, available on YouTube, you see a crowd that, as soon as the leader appears, coming out of a public building, starts shouting his name almost in unison: "Salvini, Salvini!" More than celebrating his power or expressing enthusiastic approval, the crowd wants, first and foremost, to attract his attention. They want a good framing in which to photograph him with the smartphones they are brandishing. Arms that go up with telephone in hand, simultaneously, as if they were the arms of a single body. As if this body, at whose thousand extremities appear cellphones, were acting in a peculiar performance. The excited crowd mimetically comprises a choreography, an orderly and coordinated arrangement of gestures and clicks from the photographs, indeed quite peculiar, but by now familiar. As Carozzi suggests, we are not yet, however, at the culminating moment of the event. The culmination is the selfie. The leader descends into the crowd and, in turn, putting himself in position and managing the waiting line, allows everyone to immortalize the moment in a picture with him. The faces have a smile more blissful than forced. A kind of happiness, an intense satisfaction, the tangible proof of a self-realization. There is, in the scene, a naturalness that surpasses the artificiality of the device: as if it were an extension of the body, the technological means is incorporated in the gesture, naturalized. There are also, of course, handshakes, pats on the back, and hugs, residue of old habits of a time gone by, when the culmination of the connection between the leader and the crowd lay in touching. But touch, while still exciting, appears today for what it is: transitory, fleeting, and brief, recountable but not transmissible. The image of the selfie is instead forever and, publicized on social networks, it is immediately everywhere. Although the ceremony is collective, one egotistically obtains something for oneself, or rather, one obtains a self in lasting form, shared online and thus hypervisible, in the photograph that immortalizes one's personal connection—an intimate one—with the leader. Almost as if narcissistic individualism were, today and paradoxically, the structural element of the masses.

In fact, one hesitates to call it a mass, and there are even good reasons to not call it a crowd. If anything, it is a particular crowd, surprisingly choreographic, emotionally synchronized, composed of narcissistic subjects that highlight their individuality. An individuality that places itself next to others, imitating the same gestures and nursing the same desires, but that, in the moment of enjoyment, of solemnizing the relationship between the self and the leader, remains isolated and unrelated, entirely concentrated on the act of self-immortalization. One also hesitates to qualify it as a genuinely political crowd, because the modality of its behavior, beyond the political passions that can excite it, is not at all born in the political ambit, but rather has notoriously its model in the relationship of fans with celebrities of the entertainment world, of television, cinema, and pop music. In the age of personalized politics and social media, that is, in the age of the continuous spectacularization of politics, the political leader is first and foremost a celebrity. He or she knows that, even when walking down the street, the "people of the selfie," lie in wait. It is a diverse and diffuse people, transnational and transgenerational. There are young and old, as well as men and women, each for oneself and yet all equal because all having in common the same desire and the same right: the right to the selfie. The so-called "horizontal society" created by social networks, intolerant of all hierarchies, nullifies them in emphasizing the personal connection with the leader, who is horizontally captured in a couple photo, or better still, in innumerable couple photos, iterated but individualized.

Believing that the concept of narcissism is too generic to define the peculiarity of the phenomenon, sociologists speak of self-branding in the form of self-displaying in a sort of "shop window."[2] Driven by the desire to appear in an image potentially visible to the entire world, that is, to carve out for oneself that online visibility that is synonymous with existence, one puts oneself on display publicly and increases the visibility of this shop window precisely by immortalizing oneself next to famous people who already enjoy a high level of self-display. Actually, the political leader, who willingly consents to selfies as an obvious element of self-promotion, is generally a very skilled user of videos shot in selfie mode, posted online to communicate with followers, so to speak, face-to-face. The primary relation between the leader and the crowd occurs substantially in the direct and individualizing form of the selfie. A "shop-windowed" relation that requires connection but does not imply a proper relationship. Indeed, what matters is the image; everything else remains in the background and works toward its obtainment. The image is the inauthentic that decides on the reality of the situation.

Barack Obama, in October 2017, during a public encounter in Chicago communicated that, contrary to his habits, he would no longer participate in the liturgy of selfies. "I found people were no longer looking me in the eye," he explained as justification, and "they approach me either like this, or like this," he added, turning his arm to snap another fake shot. If you concentrate all your attention on trying to get a picture with your smartphone, you block yourself from having a conversation with others, from recognizing them and listening to them, concluded the expresident of the United States, and above all you "contribute to what separates us rather than trying to break through" to other people.[3] The argument is convincing and, in a certain sense, perfectly makes the point. The selfie crowds are crowds that are highly individualistic and structurally unrelated. Their being together in the same space does not translate into a form of relationship and, much less, into an experience of plurality. Precisely the narcissistic emphasis on the individual self ensures that these crowds do not even translate into an indistinct and fusional mass, even if the same synchronic gestures would seem, in the end, to suggest it. It is, plausibly, an interesting example of "public intimacy," that of a subjectivity folded back on itself, which aims at documenting an intimate and personal relationship with the leader, by putting it on display for the public's eye.

There exists online an emblematic photograph, also rather strange and disconcerting, taken in September 2016 during Hillary Clinton's electoral campaign.[4] We are in Florida and Hillary Clinton, smiling, having entered the room and stepped on stage, raises her arm to greet her numerous supporters, who are separated from her by a railing to contain the crowd. This crowd is

7: Crowds with a Cellphone

Credit: Barbara Kinney/Hillary for America

mostly composed of young women who, simultaneously, turn their backs to Hillary Clinton and raise their smartphones to snap a selfie that depicts them with her. Technically, it is the separating railing that prevents her supporters from approaching the candidate to take a selfie with her in the usual way. But the solution, actually quite brilliant, of turning one's back to include oneself and her in the same frame resolves the problem. Hillary Clinton, evidently, appreciates it, because she, in turn, positions her back to the audience and, brandishing her cellphone, snaps a selfie herself.

The scene is truly disconcerting, because it not only contradicts the typical relation of corporeal proximity required by someone who takes a selfie with another person, but above all because it overturns, negates, and rebuffs the typical face-to-face relation of the crowd with the leader. The "people of the selfies" are, in this case, a people who turn their back on the leader, and who, in doing so, concretely double down on the lack of relation. The leader, in turn, imitates and reiterates the gesture. Even visually, if not dramatically, what comes to the fore, in this crowd, is the desire to immortalize an imaginary bond of public intimacy with the leader, that is, a bond that, although belied by the posture of the backs, takes form and duration—one could say: reality and substance—in that personal photograph that unrelated individuals, narcissistically excited with self-displaying, have managed to shoot by synchronizing their gesture. In fact, rather than dramatic, as it could seem to an external observer, the situation looks quite cheerful and fun. Even in this version, in which the crowd turns away from and forces the leader to greet their backs, the liturgy of selfies is a festive ceremony.

If it is true, as Ivan Carozzi says, that the phenomenon of selfies with the political leader reveals many aspects of the current relation "between power, masses, and technology," it is also true that the "collective subject" assembled in the scenes described above, more than a mass, resembles a crowd that is highly individualized and, at the same time, perfectly mimetic in its synchronic gesture of putting itself on display publicly. Certainly it is not a plurality. Proof of this lies in the fact that the very act of participating—if we truly want to still use this verb—already stripped of its character of interactive relationship, tolerates even the posture of backs, the interruption of all visual contact, face-to-face, replaced by the personal device of the screen that reflects and manufactures, materializes and immortalizes, the bond of public intimacy of each person with the leader. On the other hand, it is not by chance that the selfie crowd has its own particular, distinct phonosphere, characterized by the sound of clicks that give rhythm to the composite noise of voices, calls and comments, little shouts of joy and giggles. It is obviously not a harmony, but neither is it a cacophony, much less a pluriphony. Rather it is the loud and merry bustle of a general and individual excitement, of a kind of frenzy quite intense and yet brief: because the leader, after a while, inevitably leaves and the crowd disperses. Or it moves quickly to snap a selfie with another famous public figure who in the meantime has shown up elsewhere. It is often the cries of excitement of those who have first seen the new celebrity that function as an acoustic signal. Like the sonic slipstream of a route of shop-windowing to follow, the alerting cries of the first spotters signal to the people of the selfie the occurrence of a new opportunity to immortalize the self in an additional famous pairing. For the narcissistic individualities, the game of mirrors starts over again. Moreover, the protagonist of the entire affair is, quite clearly, the eye, with its specular games, not the ear. And there is even a very peculiar luminous choreography, a mobile and coordinated dance of lights in the alignment of small screens that light up.

It is widely believed that social media feed and promote the phenomenon of populism and are the true sign of the times. The technological novelty introduced by the selfie reshapes the neopopulist crowd in its relation with its leader, exacerbating its individualistic brand. The context would even be characterized by a notable effect of democratization, as it were, because each person, freely, configures, curates, and shoots the image of his or her public intimacy with the leader and disseminates it online. In other words, with this management, autonomous and, so to speak, creative, horizontally granted to all, of the image and of its diffusion, each person communicates with a potentially immense audience, thus replacing the power of traditional media in this area, presided over by an elite of "manipulative" experts. Taking a selfie and posting it online is technically easy, accessible to all. It is the democratic apotheosis of doing-it-yourself, without interferences and without intermediaries. The self-celebration online, the shop-windowing of the self in relation to countless others, as Arendt would perhaps note, has clearly supplanted the passion for standing out and excelling *among* others. And the new device has eventually enabled "the people of faces" to publicize their private happiness.

Notes

Preface to the English Edition

1. In consultation with Adriana Cavarero, I have employed the term *surging democracy* as a translation of the book's original title of *Democrazia sorgiva*. The Italian word *sorgiva* has a number of connotations, which are difficult to entirely convey in English. Among these are the notions of both source and origin, especially in regard to the origins of a river or a spring. Cavarero plays upon the related etymologies, which include the act of rising up, linked to insurrection, as well as the act of appearing or emerging. These various connotations come together to create a generative, affirmative vision of political interaction, figured as a surging democracy that wells up spontaneously amid a plurality of bodies assembled in the Arendtian "space of appearance." The adjective *surging* thus attempts to convey this thrust of upward energy along with the germinal quality of a democracy in its incipient stage. Cavarero unpacks the etymological implications of this term in particularly rich detail in Chapter 1. [—Trans.]

Chapter 1: The Idea of a Democracy

1. Norberto Bobbio, "La democrazia dei moderni paragonata a quella degli antichi (e a quella dei posteri)," *Teoria politica* 3 (1987): 4.

2. Ari-Elmeri Hyvonen and Charles Barbour, "In the Present Tense: Contemporary Engagements with Hannah Arendt," *Philosophy Today* 62, no. 2 (2018): 301.

3. Miguel Abensour, *Democracy Against the State* (London: Polity, 2010), 66.

4. I refer in particular to Judith Butler, *Notes Toward a Performative Theory of Assembly* (Cambridge, Mass.: Harvard University Press, 2015); Jacques Rancière, *Hatred of Democracy* (London: Verso, 2006); Miguel Abensour, *Democracy Against*

the State, and for more from Abensour, see *Hannah Arendt contro la filosofia politica?* trans. C. Dezzuto (Milan: Jaca Book, 2010).

5. See Abensour's essay, "Savage Democracy and the Principle of Anarchy," in *Democracy Against the State*, 102 ff.; see also Claude Lefort, *Democracy and Political Theory*, trans. David Macey (Cambridge: Polity Press, 1988), in which a specific chapter is dedicated to Arendt (45–55).

6. Étienne Balibar, *Cittadinanza*, trans. Fabrizio Grillenzoni (Turin: Bollati Boringhieri, 2012), 155; Chantal Mouffe, *On the Political* (London: Routledge, 2005). See also, on this subject, Martin Breaugh et al., eds., *Thinking Radical Democracy: The Return to Politics in Post-War France* (Toronto: University of Toronto Press, 2015). For an original interpretation of the concept of "agonistic democracy" see, within the U.S. context, Bonnie Honig, *Emergency Politics: Paradox, Law, Democracy* (Princeton, N.J.: Princeton University Press, 2009).

7. Abensour, *Democracy Against the State*, xxiii.

8. Hannah Arendt, *On Violence* (New York: Harcourt, 1970), 19, 22.

9. The expression appears in an important letter to Jaspers, dated March 4, 1951; see *Correspondence 1926–1969: Hannah Arendt, Karl Jaspers*, ed. Lotte Kohler and Hans Saner, trans. Robert and Rita Kimber (New York: Harcourt Brace Jovanovich, 1992), 166.

10. Hannah Arendt, *On Revolution* (London: Penguin Books, 1990), 30.

11. Hannah Arendt, "Marx and the Tradition of Western Political Thought," *Social Research* 69, no. 2 (2002): 303.

12. Arendt, *On Revolution*, 285 n. 11.

13. See Hannah Arendt, *Quaderni e diari (1950–1973)*, trans. Chantal Marazia (Vicenza: Neri Pozza, 2007), 164. I am quoting from this Italian translation of the two-volume German edition of Hannah Arendt, *Denktagebuch 1950–1973* (Munich: Piper Verlag, 2016); to my knowledge, there is no English translation of this important "notebook" written by Arendt in German.

14. Hannah Arendt, *Between Past and Future* (New York: Penguin Books, 1993), 154.

15. Hannah Arendt, *The Human Condition* (Chicago: University of Chicago Press, 1958), 176.

16. Ibid., 33.

17. Arendt, *Between Past and Future*, 5.

18. Arendt, *On Revolution*, 56.

19. Simona Forti, "Introduzione," *Hannah Arendt* (Milan: Bruno Mondadori, 1999), xxiv; from the same author see also *Hannah Arendt fra filosofia e politica* (Milan: Bruno Mondadori, 2006), 222.

20. Abensour, *Democracy Against the State*, xxv.

21. Arendt, *On Violence*, 56.

22. Ibid., 44.
23. The concept of the multitude is notoriously at the center of the works of Michael Hardt and Antonio Negri, *Empire* (Cambridge, Mass.: Harvard University Press, 2001), and *Multitude: War and Democracy in the Age of Empire* (New York: Penguin Books, 2005). It is worth pointing out, as an example of the success and the abuse of this concept, that, in his afterword to Abensour's book *Hannah Arendt contro la filosofia politica?* (171), Mario Pezzella writes: "The Arendt that emerges from Abensour's reading of her is the thinker of an insurgent and radical multitude."
24. Simona Forti, *Il totalitarismo* (Rome-Bari: Laterza, 2001), 102.
25. Claude Lefort with Paul Thibaud, "La communication démocratique," *Esprit* 9–10 (1979): 34; see Claude Lefort, *Democracy and Political Theory*, 9–44. On Lefort, see especially Miguel Abensour's essay "Savage Democracy and the Principle of Anarchy," along with Bryan Nelson's essay "Lefort, Abensour and the Question: What Is 'Savage' Democracy?" *Philosophy and Social Criticism* (2019): 1–18.
26. See Rancière, *Hatred of Democracy*, 49.
27. Ibid., 94.
28. The expression appears in an article of Rancière for the magazine *L'Express* (March 26, 2019, online version), tellingly entitled "Gilets jaunes: The Reasons for a Revolt." For a development of Rancière's position and further empowerment of its subversive element see Clare Woodford, *Disorienting Democracy: Politics of Emancipation* (London: Routledge, 2016).
29. See the Italian edition of Hannah Arendt, *Marx e la tradizione del pensiero politico occidentale*, trans. and ed. Simona Forti (Milan: Raffaello Cortina, 2016); and, in the same volume, Simona Forti, "Hannah Arendt lettrice di Karl Marx," 7–31.
30. Arendt, *Between Past and Future*, 169.
31. See Abensour, *Democracy Against the State*, xxv–vi.
32. See Arendt, "Marx and the Tradition of Western Political Thought."
33. Arendt, *Between Past and Future*, 155.
34. Sheldon Wolin, "Hannah Arendt: Democracy and the Political," in *Hannah Arendt. Critical Essays*, ed. Lewis P. Hinchman and Sandra K. Hinchman (Albany: State University of New York Press, 1994), 289.
35. Pier Paolo Portinaro, "La politica come cominciamento e la fine della politica," in *La politica irrappresentabile: Il pensiero politico di Hannah Arendt*, ed. Roberto Esposito (Urbino: QuattroVenti, 1987), 44.
36. Arendt, *On Violence*, 35.

Chapter 2: Plurality

This chapter is a reelaboration and expansion of my prior article: Adriana Cavarero, "Human Condition of Plurality," *Arendt Studies* 2 (2018): 37–44.

1. Hannah Arendt, *The Origins of Totalitarianism* (Orlando, Fla.: Harcourt Brace, 1994).

2. Zoe Williams, "Totalitarianism in the Age of Trump: Lessons from Hannah Arendt," *Guardian*, February 1, 2017.

3. See Jamie Bartlett, Jonathan Birdwell, and Mark Letter, *The New Face of Digital Populism* (London: Demos, 2012); Alessandro Dal Lago, *Populismo digitale* (Milan: Raffaello Cortina, 2017).

4. See Paolo Graziano, *Neopopulismi: Perché sono destinati a durare* (Bologna: Mulino, 2018), 61–76, which indicates Ernesto Laclau and Chantal Mouffe as theorists of reference for the "inclusive populism" of the radical left; Ernesto Laclau, *On Populist Reason* (London: Verso, 2007); Chantal Mouffe, *For a Left Populism* (London: Verso, 2018).

5. Graziano, *Neopopulismi*, 75, 45.

6. For a useful attempt at classification, with generous bibliography, see Jean-Paul Gagnon, Emily Beausoleil, Kyong-Min Son, Cleve Arguelles, Pierrick Chalaye, and Callum N. Johnston, "What Is Populism? Who Is the Populist?" *Democratic Theory* 5, no. 2 (2018): vi–xxvi.

7. Paolo Gerbaudo, "Populism 2.0: Social Media Activism, the Generic Internet User, and Interactive Direct Democracy," in *Social Media, Politics, and the State. Protests, Revolutions, Riots, Crime, and Policing in the Age of Facebook, Twitter, and YouTube*, ed. Daniel Trottier and Christian Fuchs (New York: Taylor & Francis, 2014), 67–87.

8. Dal Lago, *Populismo digitale*, 106.

9. Graziano, *Neopopulismi*, 45.

10. Alice Marwick and Rebecca Lewis, "Media Manipulation and Disinformation Online," *Data and Society*, May 15, 2017, https://datasociety.net/pubs/oh/DataAndSociety_Media ManipulationAndDisinformationOnline.pdf (accessed January 14, 2021).

11. Massimiliano Panarari, *Uno non vale uno: Democrazia diretta e altri miti d'oggi* (Venice: Marsilio, 2018), 63. [The term has a pejorative connotation in modern Italian, often used in reference to the people as rabble or riffraff.—Trans.]

12. Arendt, *Origins of Totalitarianism*, 314.

13. Margaret Canovan, *Hannah Arendt: A Reinterpretation of Her Political Thought* (Cambridge: Cambridge University Press, 1994), 281.

14. See Hannah Arendt, "Socrates," in *The Promise of Politics*, ed. Jerome Kohn (New York: Schocken, 2005), 5–39.

15. Hannah Arendt, *The Human Condition* (Chicago: University of Chicago Press, 1958), 8, 176, 247.

16. Ibid., 176.

17. Judith Butler, *Notes Toward a Performative Theory of Assembly* (Cambridge, Mass.: Harvard University Press, 2015), 76.
18. Arendt, *Human Condition*, 179.
19. Hannah Arendt, *On Revolution* (London: Penguin Books, 1990), 31.
20. Claude Lefort, *Democracy and Political Theory*, trans. David Macey (Cambridge: Polity Press, 1988), 51.
21. Ibid.
22. Dal Lago, *Populismo digitale*, 130–31.
23. Arendt, *Human Condition*, 52.
24. Glauco Giostra, "La trappola del pensiero liofilizzato," *La lettura* literary supplement to *Corriere della sera*, February 10, 2019, 9.
25. Arendt, *On Revolution*, 165–68.
26. See Shmuel Lederman, *Hannah Arendt and Participatory Democracy. A People Utopia* (London: Palgrave Macmillan, 2019).
27. Hannah Arendt, *On Violence* (New York: Harcourt, 1970), 6, 85.
28. Ibid., 41, 51.
29. Simona Forti, *Hannah Arendt fra filosofia e politica* (Milan: Bruno Mondadori, 2006), 5.
30. See *Correspondence 1926–1969: Hannah Arendt, Karl Jaspers*, ed. Lotte Kohler and Hans Saner, trans. Robert and Rita Kimber (New York: Harcourt Brace Jovanovich, 1992),166.
31. Arendt, *Human Condition*, 198.
32. Ibid., 199.
33. See Forti, *Hannah Arendt fra filosofia e politica*, 271–72.
34. Arendt, *Human Condition*, 188.

Chapter 3: Public Happiness

1. Hannah Arendt, *The Human Condition* (Chicago: University of Chicago Press, 1958), 38.
2. Ibid.
3. Hannah Arendt, *On Revolution* (London: Penguin Books, 1990), 124.
4. Ibid., 127.
5. Ibid., 130.
6. Ibid., 131.
7. Ibid., 119.
8. Ibid., 120.
9. Ibid., 119.
10. Elisabeth Young-Bruehl, *Hannah Arendt: For Love of the World* (New Haven, Conn.: Yale University Press, 1982), 404.

11. Eugenia Lamedica, *Hannah Arendt e il '68: Fra politica e violenza* (Milan: Jaca Book, 2018), 14.

12. Hannah Arendt, "Thoughts on Politics and Revolution," in *Crisis of the Republic* (New York: Harcourt Brace, 1972), 202.

13. Ibid., 206.

14. Hannah Arendt, *On Violence* (New York: Harcourt, 1970), 19, 23.

15. Ibid., 74.

16. Michael Gottsegen, *The Political Thought of Hannah Arendt* (Albany: State University of New York Press, 1994). The following quotations are all taken from p. ix.

17. Lynne Segal, *Radical Happiness: Moments of Collective Joy* (London: Verso, 2017), 206–7.

18. Olivia Guaraldo, "Public Happiness: Revisiting an Arendtian Hypothesis," *Philosophy Today* 62, no. 2 (2018): 412.

19. Ibid., 413.

20. Hannah Arendt, "The Freedom to Be Free," in *Thinking Without a Bannister. Essays in Understanding (1953–1975)*, ed. Jerome Khon (New York: Schocken, 2018), 384.

21. Arendt, *On Violence*, 7.

22. Arendt, *Human Condition*, 176.

23. See Aristotle, *Nicomachean Ethics* X.1178.

24. Arendt, *Human Condition*, 193.

25. Ibid.

26. See Aristotle, *Politics* 1253a.

27. Hannah Arendt, *Between Past and Future* (New York: Penguin Books, 1993), 22.

28. See Aristotle, *Politics* 1252b.

29. I have treated this uncomfortable subject in my essay "Ombre aristoteliche sulla lettura arendtiana di Marx," in Hannah Arendt, *Marx e la tradizione del pensiero politico occidentale*, trans. and ed. Simona Forti (Milan: Raffaello Cortina, 2016), 142–62.

30. John Kiess, *Hannah Arendt and Theology* (London: Bloomsbury, 2016), 173.

31. Arendt, *Human Condition*, 206.

32. Ibid., 207.

33. See Jeremy Bentham, *An Introduction to the Principles of Morals and Legislation* (New York: Dover Publications, 2007).

34. Alexis de Tocqueville, *Democracy in America* (Chicago: University of Chicago Press, 2000), 663.

35. For a wider and interesting analysis, see Emanuele Felice, *Storia economica della felicità* (Bologna: Mulino, 2017), in which he links the economic development to the

Notes

fabric of social relations, to the "meaning of life" for the individual and the collectivity, and, not least, to the sphere of rights. But see also, in order to get an idea of the framework for this stream of studies, Bruno S. Frey, Alois Stutzer, *Happiness and Economics: How the Economy and Institutions Affect Well-Being* (Princeton, N.J.: Princeton University Press, 2002); Derek Bok, *The Politics of Happiness: What Government Can Learn from the New Research on Well-Being* (Princeton, N.J.: Princeton University Press, 2010).

36. Arendt, *Human Condition*, 133.

37. Exemplary, in this sense, is Raymond Guess's article "Happiness and Politics" (in *Arion. A Journal of Humanities and the Classics* 10 (2002): 15–33), which, using a text from Saint-Just, reexamines the concept of "public happiness" from various well-documented perspectives, among which, however, Arendt's perspective does not appear.

Chapter 4: Political Squares

1. Hisham Matar, *The Return: Fathers, Sons and the Land in Between* (London: Penguin Books, 2017).

2. All quotes are taken from ibid., 110–12.

3. Judith Butler, *Notes Toward a Performative Theory of Assembly* (Cambridge, Mass.: Harvard University Press, 2015), 136.

4. For a useful comparative study see *Street Politics in the Age of Austerity: From the Indignados to Occupy*, ed. Marco Ancelovici, Pascale Dufour, and Héloise Nez (Amsterdam: Amsterdam University Press, 2016).

5. See the illuminating essay by Héloise Nez, "'We Must Register a Victory to Continue Fighting': Locating the Action of the Indignados in Madrid," in *Street Politics in the Age of Austerity*, 121–45.

6. Butler, *Notes Toward a Performative Theory of Assembly*, 11, 20.

7. Ibid., 94.

8. Ibid., 26.

9. Ibid., 182.

10. Ibid., 52.

11. Ibid., 73.

12. Ibid., 118.

13. Ibid., 86.

14. See ibid., 96.

15. Ibid., 117.

16. Hannah Arendt, *On Revolution* (London: Penguin Books, 1990), 112–14.

17. Ibid., 109.

18. Butler, *Notes Toward a Performative Theory of Assembly*, 47.

19. Judith Butler and Gayatri Chakravorty Spivak, *Who Sings the Nation-state? Language, Politics, Belonging* (Oxford: Seagull Books, 2007), 21.

20. Butler, *Notes Toward a Performative Theory of Assembly*, 151.
21. Ibid., 119.
22. Ibid., 76.
23. Ibid., 218.
24. Ibid., 207.
25. Ibid.
26. Ibid., 8.
27. Ibid., 91.
28. Hannah Arendt, *The Human Condition* (Chicago: University of Chicago Press, 1958), 205.
29. Ibid., 247.
30. Butler, *Notes Toward a Performative Theory of Assembly*, 187.
31. Arendt, *Human Condition*, 200.
32. See Wolfgang Heuer, "Plurality," *Arendt Studies* 2 (2018): 53–56.

Chapter 5: The Voice of the Masses

1. Judith Butler, *Notes Toward a Performative Theory of Assembly* (Cambridge, Mass.: Harvard University Press, 2015), 124.
2. Ibid.
3. Ibid.
4. Ibid.
5. Ibid., 182–83.
6. Ibid., 183.
7. Hannah Arendt, *The Origins of Totalitarianism* (Orlando, Fla.: Harcourt Brace, 1994), 311.
8. Ibid.
9. See Emilio Gentile, *Il capo e la folla* (Roma-Bari: Laterza, 2016), viii; Stefan Jonsson, *Crowds and Democracy* (New York: Columbia University Press, 2013), xix.
10. For a useful reference, see Paolo Cristofolini, "*Populus, plebs, multitudo*: Nota lessicale su alcuni interscambi e fluttuazioni di significato da Livio e Machiavelli a Spinoza," in *Laboratorio dell'ISPF* (2008), www.ispf-lab.cnr.it/system/files/ispf_lab/documenti/multitudo_cristofolini.pdf (accessed January 14, 2021).
11. Jonsson, *Crowds and Democracy*, 9.
12. Alfred Vierkandt, *Gesellschaftslehere: Hauptprobleme der philosophiscen Soziologie* (1928), quoted in Jonsson, *Crowds and Democracy*, 8; but, as evidence of the fact that the topic of the crowd is today drawing new and justified interest, see also, from the same author, *Brief History of the Masses* (New York: Columbia University Press, 2008), and Christian Borch, *The Politics of Crowds: An Alternative History of Sociology* (New York: Cambridge University Press, 2012).
13. Gustave Le Bon, *La psychologie des foules* (Paris: Presses Universitaires de France, 2003), 19.

Notes

14. Elias Canetti, *Crowds and Power*, trans. Carol Stewart (New York: Continuum, 1978), 80.

15. Ibid., 80–81. Here and elsewhere, in the quotations of Canetti's texts, the italics appear in the original.

16. Ibid., 35.

17. Elias Canetti, *The Memoirs of Elias Canetti* (New York: Farrar, Straus & Giroux, 2000). This one-volume edition includes the three autobiographical books of Canetti: *The Tongue Set Free*, *The Torch in My Ear*, *The Play of the Eyes*. They cover his life from 1905 to 1937.

18. Ibid., 407.

19. Ibid., 484–85.

20. Ibid., 489.

21. See the important and disquieting reflections of Nidesh Lawtoo: *(New) Fascism: Contagion, Community, Myth* (East Lansing: Michigan State University Press, 2019).

22. Canetti, *Memoirs of Elias Canetti*, 487.

23. Ibid., 492.

24. Ibid., 492–93.

25. Susan Sontag, *Under the Sign of Saturn* (New York: Vintage Books, 1980), 196.

26. Canetti, *Memoirs of Elias Canetti*, 493.

27. Butler, *Notes Toward a Performative Theory of Assembly*, 166.

28. Ibid., 175–76.

29. Ibid., 175.

30. Ibid., 179, 181.

31. Hannah Arendt, *On Revolution* (London: Penguin Books, 1990), 94.

32. See Gentile, *Il capo e la folla*, 78, 100.

33. See George L. Mosse, *Confronting the Nations: Jewish and Western Nationalism* (Hanover, N.H.: Brandeis University Press, 1993), 23.

34. I take these and all following quotes, referring to the same text, from the online version, at the site www.writingshome.com, from Emile Zola's *The Fortune of the Rougons*, 23–25.

35. Boris Pasternak, *Doctor Zhivago*, trans. Max Hayward and Manya Harari (New York: Pantheon Books, 1958), 35.

Chapter 6: The Voice of Plurality

1. This and all following quotations are taken from Hannah Arendt, "The Hungarian Revolution and Totalitarian Imperialism," in Hannah Arendt, *Thinking Without a Bannister: Essays in Understanding (1953–1975)*, (New York: Schocken, 2018), 129.

2. Hannah Arendt, *The Origins of Totalitarianism* (Orlando, Fla.: Harcourt Brace, 1994), 467.

3. I have developed this subject in Adriana Cavarero, *For More Than One Voice: Toward a Philosophy of Vocal Expression*, trans. Paul A. Kottman (Stanford, Calif.: Stanford University Press, 2005), 210 ff.

4. Elias Canetti, *The Voices of Marrakesh: A Record of a Visit*, trans. J. A. Underwood (New York: Penguin Books, 2012), 44.

5. Elias Canetti, *The Memoirs of Elias Canetti* (New York: Farrar, Straus and Giroux, 2000), 493.

6. Canetti, *Voices of Marrakesh*, 17.

7. Ibid., 18–19.

8. Ibid., 106–9.

9. Anne Fuchs, "'The Deeper Nature of My German': Mother Tongue, Subjectivity, and the Voice of the Other in Elias Canetti's Autobiography," in *A Companion to the Works of Elias Canetti*, ed. Dagmar C. G. Lorenz (Rochester, N.Y.: Camden House, 2004), 58.

10. Kata Gellen, "The Opaque Voice: Canetti's Foreign Tongue," in *The World of Elias Canetti: Centenary Essays*, ed. William Collins Donahue and Julian Preece (Newcastle: Cambridge Scholars Publishing, 2007), 25.

11. Susan Sontag, *Under the Sign of Saturn* (New York: Vintage Books, 1980), 196, 197.

12. Canetti, *Memoirs of Elias Canetti*, 417.

13. Ibid., 497.

14. Ibid., 47.

15. Ibid., 30.

16. Ibid., 33.

17. Canetti, *The Voices of Marrakesh*, 45.

18. Ibid.

19. Roland Barthes, *The Rustle of Language*, trans. Richard Howard (Berkeley: University of California Press, 1989). The essay "Le bruissement de la langue" came out in 1975 and then was included in the collection of essays that appeared under the same name for the Éditions du Seuil in 1984. The first edition of Canetti's *Die Stimmen von Marrakesch* is from 1968.

20. Barthes, *Rustle of Language*, 76. All the quotations that follow are taken from the short essay on pp. 76–78.

21. Judith Butler, *Notes Toward a Performative Theory of Assembly* (Cambridge, Mass.: Harvard University Press, 2015), 124.

22. Sontag, *Under the Sign of Saturn*, 196.

23. Canetti, *Memoirs of Elias Canetti*, 556.

24. Ibid., 673.

25. Ibid., 678.

26. Ibid., 689.

Chapter 7: Crowds with a Cellphone

1. Ivan Carozzi, "Preparate i telefoni," *Il Post*, January 8, 2019, www.ilpost.it/?blog_post=preparate-i-telefoni (accessed January 14, 2021).
2. See Vanni Codeluppi, *Mi metto in vetrina: Selfie, Facebook, Apple, Hello Kitty, Renzi e altre "vetrinizzazioni"* (Milan: Mimesis, 2015).
3. See the online article by Rica Demarest, "Obama Doesn't Want To Take a Selfie with You, and This Is Why," in *The Block Club*, October 31, 2017, www.dnainfo.com/chicago/20171031/south-loop/barack-michelle-obama-summit-selfie-president (accessed January 14, 2021).
4. See www.repubblica.it/speciali/esteri/presidenziali-usa2016/2016/09/26/foto/usa_campagna_nell_era_del_selfie_la_folla_volta_le_spalle_a_hillary-148550124/1/#1 (accessed January 14, 2021).

Index

Page numbers in *italics* indicate illustrations.

Abensour, Miguel, 4, 9, 10, 12, 99n23
Adams, John, 32, 37, 41
agonistic democracy, 4, 6, 12, 98n6
agorà, 3, 7, 22, 23, 33, 40, 55, 85
American Revolution: democracy and, 8; plurality and, 24–25, 28; public happiness and, 31–33, 36–37, 41, 50
anarchic democracy, 4, 10–11
Annual Happiness Report (United Nations), 43
Antonioni, Michelangelo, 80
Arab Spring, 45–46, 47, 53
Arendt, Hannah: *Denktagebuch (Quaderni e diari)*, 98n13; *The Freedom to be Free*, 36–37; *The Human Condition*, 7, 15, 18–19, 25, 27, 33, 37, 38; "The Hungarian Revolution and Totalitarian Imperialism," 72; *The Origins of Totalitarianism*, 7, 15, 18, 29; *Between Past and Future*, v; *On Revolution*, 5, 25, 31, 33, 35, 36, 37, 44, 50; *On Violence*, 25. See also political thought of Hannah Arendt
Aristotle, 27, 37, 39–41, 52, 102n29
assembly form of political action. *See* public squares

Balibar, Étienne, 4
Barthes, Roland, 75, 80–82, 84, 106n19
Belgium, George Floyd protests in, xiv
"Bella Ciao," x, xi
Benjamin, Walter, xiv
Bentham, Jeremy, 41, 43
Bergson, Henri, 34
Berlin, Germany, George Floyd protests in, xiv
Between Past and Future (Arendt), v
Black Bloc movement, 59
Black Lives Matter, xiv–xvi
Bobbio, Norberto, 3, 6
Bok, Derek, 103n35
Bolzano (Italy), quality of life/happiness ratio in, 42

109

Bonaparte, Louis-Napoléon, 69
Borch, Christian, 104n9
Bristol, England, George Floyd protests in, xiv
Brock, Hermann, 83
Butler, Judith: on multitudes/masses/crowds, 59–60, 66–67; *Notes Toward a Performative Theory of Assembly*, 46, 47, 51, 53, 54; political thought of Arendt and, xi, xv, 4, 20, 48–55; public happiness and, 53; on public squares, 46–56, 85; on speech, 52–53; on violence, 54; on voice of plurality, 75, 82–83, 85; *Who Sings the Nation-State? Language, Politics, Belonging* (Butler and Spivak), 50–51

Cairo, Egypt, Tahrir Square in, 47
Canetti, Elias, 62, 63–67, 70, 75–85
Canovan, Margaret, 19
Carozzi, Ivan, 89–90, 94
cellphones, crowds, and leaders, 89–95, 93
Chung Kuo-Cina (Antonioni film, 1973), 80–81
civil disobedience/civil rights/student movement (1960s), 9, 33–34
Clinton, Hilary, 89, 92–93, 93
Codeluppi, Vanni, 107n2
collective identity, Arendt's aversion to, 26
Colston, Edward, xiv
Comedy of Vanity (Canetti), 84
Constitution, US, 66
consumerism and happiness, 42–43
coronavirus/COVID-19 pandemic, xi–xiii
creative violence, 11, 29, 34, 35
Cristofolini, Paolo, 104n10
crowds. *See* multitudes/masses/crowds

Crowds and Power (Canetti), 63–64, 77

Dal Lago, Alessandro, 17
Demarest, Rica, 107n3
democracy: absence of rule, association with, 5–6, 9–10; avoidance of term by Arendt, 5, 6, 13, 18–19; as idea, 3–5; as politics, for Arendt, 5, 6. *See also specific types or descriptions, e.g.* surging democracy
Democracy in America (Tocqueville), 42
Denktagebuch (Quaderni e diari; Arendt), 98n13
Di Maio, Luigi, 89
digital populism, 15–19, 22–24, 27
direct democracy, 3, 18–19, 23, 25
Doctor Zhivago (Pasternak), 70–71
dokei moi, 19

e-democracy, 16, 18
energeia, 41
equality, 21–22
eu zen, 40–41
eudaimonia, 39–41

Felice, Emanuele, 102–3n35
felicity, 38–40
feminine characteristics attributed to crowds, 63
feminism and feminist movement, 36, 43–44, 48
Finland, happiness quotient in, 42
Five Star Movement, 16–17
Floyd, George, murder of, and ensuing protests, xiii–xvi
Forti, Simona, 8–9, 25, 99n24, 99n29
The Fortune of the Rougons (Zola), 69–70, 74
The Freedom to be Free (Arendt), 36–37
freedom/liberation: economic need, distinguished from domain of,

Index

50; plurality and, 21, 28; political thought of Arendt and, 5, 8, 9
French Revolution, 8, 28, 50, 65, 67–68
Freud, Sigmund, 62, 64, 70
Fuchs, Anne, 106n9

Gaddafi, Muamar, 45
Gellen, Kata, 106n10
Gentile, Emilio, 104n9
Gerbaudo, Paolo, 100n7
Germany: George Floyd protests in, xiv; Workers' Councils (1918), 9
Gezi Park, Istanbul, 47
Global Climate Strike (March 2019), 44
Giostra, Claudio, 101n24
Gordon, Ibby, 77
Gottsegen, Michael, 35
Graziano, Paolo, 100n4
the Gracchi, 61
Greek *agorà*, 3, 7, 22, 23, 33, 40, 55, 85
Greek concept of democracy/politics, 3, 5–8, 14, 50–51, 53
Guaraldo, Olivia, 36
The Guardian, 15
Guess, Raymond, 103n37

happiness: consumerism and, 42–43; individual or private versus public, 30–31, 41. *See also* public happiness
Hardt, Michael, 99n23
hate speech, 23
Hegel, Georg Wilhelm Friedrich, 81
Herodotus, 5
Heuer, Wolfgang, 104n32
Hobbes, Thomas, 14, 62
Honig, Bonnie, xi, 98n6
The Human Condition (Arendt), 7, 15, 18–19, 25, 27, 33, 37, 38
Hungarian Revolution, 9, 33
"The Hungarian Revolution and Totalitarian Imperialism" (Arendt), 72

immigration, xiv–xv, 17
Indignados, in Spain, 46–47
individual or private happiness: cellphones, crowds, and leaders, 89–95, 93; public happiness versus, 30–31, 41
individualism, networked, 18
insurgent democracy, 4, 9, 10, 11–12, 28–29
isonomy *(isonomia)*, 5–6
Istanbul, Gezi Park in, 47
Italian experience of 2021, ix–xvi

Jefferson, Thomas, 32, 33, 37, 41
Jonsson, Stefan, 104n9, n11
Journal of Happiness, 43

Khon, Jerome, 36
Kiess, John, 40–41

Laclau, Ernesto, 100n4
Lamedica, Eugenia, 102n11
Lawtoo, Nidesh, 105n21
Le Bon, Gustave, 62, 63, 64, 70
leadership and crowds, 63, 65, 89–95
Lederman, Shmuel, 101n26
Lefort, Claude, 4, 10
Lega Party, ix, 89
Leopold II (king of Belgium), xiv
liberalism, xv, 5, 13, 15, 23, 42, 43, 48
liberation. *See* freedom/liberation
Libya, Arab Spring in, 45–46, 53
"ludic" nature of plurality, 27–28

makarios, 39, 40
March for Our Lives (March 2018), 43–44
Marek, Thomas, 83
"La Marseillaise," 68–70
Marxism, 11, 12, 13, 34, 62
masses. *See* multitudes/masses/crowds
Matar, Hisham, 45–46

Al-Mayadin (newspaper), 46
media. *See* technology and social media
The Memoirs of Elias Canetti, 64–65, 78, 105n17
Mosse, George, 68
Mouffe, Chantal, 4, 100n4
multitudes/masses/crowds, 59–71; Butler on, 59–60, 66–67; Canetti on, 62, 63–67, 70; concept of, 10, 99n23; defined, 62–63; etymology of, 61; leadership and, 63, 65, 89–95; modern scholarship on, 62–67; negative and positive uses of, 61–62; plurality versus, 55–56, 60, 61, 63, 66–68; in political thought of Arendt, 60–61; political thought of Arendt on, 67–68; singing, 68–70; voice of, 64–71
Musil, Robert, 83, 84

natality, 19, 36–39, 85
nation-states, 25–26, 50–51, 54
Nazis and Nazism, xiv, 68
Negri, Antonio, 99n23
Nelson, Bryan, 99n25
neoliberalism, 13, 48
neo-plebs, 18, 100n11
neopopulism, 15
networked individualism, 18
Neue Freie Presse, 78
New York Times, xiii, 30
Nez, Héloïse, 103n5
Notes Toward a Performative Theory of Assembly (Butler), 46, 47, 51, 53, 54

Obama, Barack, 89, 92
Occupy Wall Street movement, 47, 66
On Revolution (Arendt), 5, 25, 31, 33, 35, 36, 37, 44, 50
On Violence (Arendt), 25
The Origins of Totalitarianism (Arendt), 7, 15, 18, 29

Panari, Massimiliano, 100n11
Paris Commune, 9
Pasternak, Boris, 70–71, 72
Peronism, 17
Pezzella, Mario, 99n23
Plato, 6, 7, 8, 10, 61
plurality, 15–29; collective identity, Arendt's aversion to, 26–27; conflict accompanying, 13–14; digital populism, problem of, 15–19, 22–24, 27, 29; freedom/equality and, 21–22; freedom/liberation and, 21, 28; as human condition, 19–20; institutional issues, freedom from, 24–26; "ludic" nature of, 27–28; multitudes/masses/crowds versus, 55–56, 60, 61, 63, 66–68; politics as plural interaction within shared space, Arendt's view of, 4–8, 11, 19–21; public happiness and, 37–38, 44; public squares and, 48–49, 51–56; qualitative versus quantitative approach to, 55; revolution and, 28; "space of appearance" and, 26; surging democracy and, 26, 29. *See also* voice of plurality
pluriphony, as voice of plurality, 75, 81, 83
political thought of Hannah Arendt, 3–14; centrality to current concepts of politics/democracy, 4–5, 9, 10–11; conflict in, 13–14; freedom/liberation and, 5, 8, 9; governing process, politics viewed as, 7–8; Italian experience in 2021 and, ix–xvi; plural interaction within shared space, Arendt's view of politics as, 4–8, 11, 19–21; power/violence and, 9, 14 (*See also* power; violence); revolution and, 8–10; surging democracy, concept of, x, 11–12; utopian impulse of Arendtian perspective

on, 13–14. *See also* democracy; multitudes/masses/crowds; plurality; public squares
Politics (Aristotle), 40
politics of the street. *See* public squares
Pollock, Griselda, 15
Portinaro, Pier Paolo, 13–14
Il Post, 89
power: cellphones, crowds, and leaders, 89–95, *93*; plurality and, 25, 55; violence and, 9, 14, 33, 53–54
Prague Spring/Velvet Revolution, 33, 35, 36
private and public realms, Arendtian distinction of, 48–49, 52
private or individual happiness: cellphones, crowds, and leaders, 89–95, *93*; public happiness versus, 30–31, 41
The Psychology of Crowds (Le Bon), 63
public happiness, 30–44; Aristotelian political thought and, 37, 39–41; Butler and, 53; consumerism versus, 42–43; etymological connections, 38–41; individual or private happiness versus, 30–31, 41; modern Arendtian experiences of, 33–34, 43–44; natality and, 36–39; plurality and, 37–38, 44; revolution and discovery of, 31–37, 50; in "Sardine" movement, x, xi; as shared action, 34; surging democracy and, 29; utilitarianism/happiness-maximization versus, 41–42, 43; voice of plurality as tone of, 82
Public Life (newspaper), 33
public squares, 45–56; *agorà*, 3, 7, 22, 23, 33, 40, 55, 85; Arendt versus Butler on, 48–55; Butler on, 46–56, 85; modern examples of phenomenon of, 45–47; plurality and, 48–49, 51–56

Putin, Vladimir, 89

racial protests following murder of George Floyd, xiii–xvi
radical democracy, 4
Radical Happiness: Moments of Collective Joy (Segal), 35–36
Rancière, Jacques, 4, 10–11, 99n28
Renzi, Matteo, 89
representative democracy, 3, 16, 24
The Return: Fathers, Son, and the Land in Between (Matar), 45–46
revolution: public happiness, discovery of, 31–37, 50; rediscovery of politics and, 8–10, 28. *See also specific revolutions*
Rousseau, Jean Jacques, 67
Rousseau platform, 16–17
Russian Revolution, 9
The Rustle of Language (Barthes), 80–82, 84, 106n19

Salvini, Matteo, ix, xv, 89–90
"Sardines" movement in Italy, ix–xi, xv
Segal, Lynne, 35–36
selfies, crowds, and leaders, 89–95, *93*
Sermon on the Mount, 39
singing, mass, 68–70
smartphones, crowds, and leaders, 89–95, *93*
social distancing, xi–xiii
social media. *See* technology and social media
Socrates, 19
sonority. *See* vocality/sonority
Sontag, Susan, 65–66, 77, 83
space of appearance, 26, 48–52, 55
Spain, Indignados in, 46–47
speech, Butler versus Arendt on, 52–53. *See also specific entries at* vocal/voice

Spinoza, Baruch, 62
statues, George Floyd protests and removal of, xiv–xv
street, politics of the. *See* public squares
student movement of 1960s, 9, 33–34
surging democracy, x, 11–12, 26, 29, 36, 59, 85

Tahrir Square, Cairo, Egypt, 47
technology and social media: crowd and leader, relationship between, 89–95, 93; digital populism, 15–19, 22–24, 27
Terbil, Fatih, 45
theater: as political art, 27, 41; voice of plurality in, 84
Thucydides, 25
Tocqueville, Alexis de, 42
The Tongue Set Free (Canetti), 78–79
totalitarianism, 7, 9, 10, 14, 18, 25, 60–62, 68, 70, 72–74
Trento (Italy), quality of life/happiness ratio in, 42
true democracy, 4
Trump, Donald, 15, 89

uniqueness, 26, 83–84
United Nations, 43
University of California, Berkeley, 30, 33
utilitarianism and happiness-maximization, 41–42, 43

Velvet Revolution/Prague Spring, 33, 35, 36
Verona, Italy, George Floyd protests in, xiv

Vierkandt, Alfred, 104n12
violence: Butler on, 54; creative, 11, 29, 34, 35; power and, 9, 14, 33, 53–54; student movement's glorification of, 34
vocal uniqueness, 83–84
vocality/sonority: Butler versus Arendt on speech, 52–53; multitudes/masses/crowds, voice of, 64–71
voice of plurality, 72–85; Barthes on, 75, 80–82, 84; Butler on, 75, 82–83, 85; Canetti on, 75–85; childhood and natality, 84–85; Pasternak poem, group recitation of, 72–75; as pluriphony, 75, 81, 83; public happiness, tone of, 82; in theater, 84
The Voices of Marrakesh (Canetti), 75–76, 77, 79–80, 81, 82, 84–85

Weber, Max, 14, 62
Who Sings the Nation-State? Language, Politics, Belonging (Butler and Spivak), 50–51
wild (savage) democracy, 4, 10
"will of the people," 17
Williams, Zoe, 15
Wolin, Sheldom, 13
Women's March (January 2017), 43–44
Woodford, Clare, 99n28
World Happiness Day, 43

Yale University, 30
Yellow Vest movement, 59
Young-Bruehl, Elisabeth, 33
YouTube, 90

Zola, Émile, 69, 74

The authorized representative in the EU for product safety and compliance is:
Mare Nostrum Group
B.V Doelen 72
4831 GR Breda
The Netherlands

www.ingramcontent.com/pod-product-compliance
Lightning Source LLC
Chambersburg PA
CBHW031435150426
43191CB00006B/524